About Island Press

Island Press is the only nonprofit organization in the United States whose principal purpose is the publication of books on environmental issues and natural resource management. We provide solutions-oriented information to professionals, public officials, business and community leaders, and concerned citizens who are shaping responses to environmental problems.

In 1994, Island Press celebrated its tenth anniversary as the leading provider of timely and practical books that take a multidisciplinary approach to critical environmental concerns. Our growing list of titles reflects our commitment to bringing the best of an expanding body of literature to the environmental community throughout North America and the world.

Support for Island Press is provided by The Geraldine R. Dodge Foundation, The Energy Foundation, The Ford Foundation, William and Flora Hewlett Foundation, The James Irvine Foundation, The John D. and Catherine T. MacArthur Foundation, The Andrew W. Mellon Foundation, The Pew Charitable Trusts, The Rockefeller Brothers Fund, The Tides Foundation, Turner Foundation, Inc., The Rockefeller Philanthropic Collaborative, Inc., and individual donors.

About the Rural Economic Policy Program

Established in 1985, the Rural Economic Policy Program (REPP) fosters collaborative learning and innovation to advance rural community and economic development in the United States. REPP aims to help rural decisionmakers better understand how local choices and opportunities fit into the larger economy, and to speed the adoption of a comprehensive set of public and private initiatives that will sustain rural progress and improve the lives of rural people. Headquartered at The Aspen Institute in Washington, D.C., REPP is funded by the Ford and W.K. Kellogg Foundations. The Aspen Institute is an international organization whose programs enhance the ability of leaders in business, government, the nonprofit sector, academia, and the media to understand and act upon the issues that challenge the national and international community. ´

For more information about REPP or REPP publications, please write to: Rural Economic Policy Program, The Aspen Institute, 1333 New Hampshire Avenue, NW, Suite 1070, Washington, DC 20036. Or call REPP Program Assistant Diane Morton at (202) 736-5804.

Guide to Rural Data

Revised Edition

Guide to Rural Data

Revised Edition

Priscilla Salant and Anita J. Waller

Rural Economic Policy Program
of The Aspen Institute

ISLAND PRESS

Washington, D.C. ❑ Covelo, California

Library of Congress Cataloging-in-Publication Data

Salant, Priscilla.
　　Guide to rural data / Priscilla Salant and Anita J. Waller.—
Rev. ed.
　　　　p.　　cm.
　　Rev. ed. of: A community researcher's guide to rural data /
Priscilla Salant. ©1990.
　　Includes bibliographical references and index.
　　ISBN 1-55963-384-0 (alk. paper)
　　1. Rural population—United States—Statistical services.
2. United States—Rural conditions—Statistics. 3. Community
development—United States. 4. Rural development—United States.
I. Waller, Anita J. II. Salant, Priscilla. Community researcher's
guide to rural data. III. Title.
HB2385.S26　1995
330.973'009173'4—dc20　　　　　　　　　　　　　　95-23376
　　　　　　　　　　　　　　　　　　　　　　　　　　CIP

Printed on recycled, acid-free paper

Manufactured in the United States of America
10 9 8 7 6 5 4 3 2 1

Contents

Introduction

1
Data Concepts

2
Overview of Sources

3

Characterizing Local Population and Community Resources

4

Understanding the Economies of Rural Communities

5

Analyzing Government in Rural Communities

Glossary 97

Appendices 103

References   129

Index   133

List of Tables and Figures

Tables

Figures

Acknowledgments

The first edition of this book, *A Community Researcher's Guide to Rural Data,* was funded by a grant from the Rural Poverty and Resources Program of The Ford Foundation with assistance from the Rural Economic Policy Program (REPP) of The Aspen Institute. The revised edition was funded with support from The Kellogg Foundation, again with help from REPP. We gratefully acknowledge the generous financial support from each of these organizations and their staffs (present and former). They include Norm Collins, Cynthia Duncan, Meriwether Jones, and Susan Sechler.

In addition, the authors would like to thank the patient and dedicated employees of Federal agencies who answered our innumerable questions. People at the Census Bureau (especially in the Denver Regional Office) and the Bureau of Economic Analysis gave us public service at its very best.

Many reviewers and others provided thoughtful comments on the first edition, and we kept their suggestions in mind as we made our revisions. They include Peggy Adams, Paul Barkley, Henry Carey, Annabel Cook, Ron Faas, Peggy Ross Cook, Richard Salant, Barbara Smith, Marty Strange, and Kathryn Wallman. Deb Schwenson in the Department of Agricultural Economics at Washington State University provided invaluable help with the logistics of preparing a final draft. Thanks also to the staff of the Denver Card Company for their excellent service.

Special thanks are due to Roger Sonnichsen for his support and for graciously living with the project after it exceeded the bounds of the home office. Thanks also to Deloris and Tom Waller for years of encouragement and enthusiasm. Finally, thanks to the following people for their time when they had better things to do: Kay Chapman, Brenda Jepsen, George Gunn, and Dennis Waller.

Introduction

The first edition of this book, *A Community Researcher's Guide to Rural Data,* was prepared at the request of the Rural Economic Policy Program of The Aspen Institute and supported with funds from The Ford Foundation. Staff from both organizations recognize that reliable and timely data are a prerequisite for sound planning and development policy. Unfortunately, decision makers in rural communities are often hampered in their work because they don't know that such data exist or where to find them.

Hence, our purpose in writing this book is to acquaint researchers with data they can use to describe and better understand rural communities. We have written primarily for people in locally based organizations, but we hope that researchers in universities, state government, and policy institutes will also find the book useful.

Background

Rural America has experienced dramatic demographic and economic changes in the last several decades. During the 1960s and '70s, population and employment in rural communities grew and the long-standing gap between rural and urban incomes became smaller. Just when many analysts were predicting an economic revival in rural America, the fortunes turned and news from the heartland became relentlessly discouraging. The income gap began to grow again and migration from rural to urban areas resumed.

Although population data from the early 1990s show that conditions are improving in many small towns, national-level statistics still tell of a rural America that lags behind the rest of the country in income and job growth. Poverty and unemployment rates are higher, education levels lower, and the effects of recession often more severe. Especially in the Midwest, many rural places are steadily losing population as people leave in search of better jobs. In small communities that have been hard hit economically and lost population, access to health care, education, and other services is often a serious problem.

People who work with and live in rural places are searching for new development models that promise more stability and prosperity than in the past. While some people still yearn for the "good old days," others agree that if rural communities are to survive—let alone prosper—they must find new

goods to produce, new services to offer, and new ways of interacting with
each other and the world around them. Many communities are making
progress toward these goals by finding new ways to cooperate, share
resources, and take advantage of savings that often come with increased size
(17).* Accomplishing these goals is an enormous challenge that requires reliable information and analysis.

Unfortunately, data collection efforts have not kept pace with changing
rural conditions. Part of the reason for the gaps in rural data is obvious: the
cost of collecting reliable statistical data increases as population becomes
more sparse. To save money, most data collection activities use sample
designs that yield more information for urban than rural areas. Sampling
rates typically used in national surveys produce enough observations to make
estimates with relatively small sampling errors in urban areas but not in rural
areas. Despite these problems, a wealth of secondary data is available to
describe rural places, people, and businesses. This book documents these
data sources for both experienced researchers and local decision makers who
are unfamiliar with statistical data.[1]

What Are "Rural" Data?

In the context of identifying data sources, "rural" is a geographic concept
based on two standards defined by Federal agencies that collect statistics.
The first standard is the urban/rural designation used by the Bureau of the
Census in its decennial count of population and housing units. According to
the Bureau's definition, an *urban* area is any incorporated or unincorporated
place with a population of at least 2,500. Everything else is *rural.*

The second standard is the metropolitan designation assigned to every
U.S. county by the Office of Management and Budget. Counties are considered *metropolitan* if they have a city with a population of at least 50,000 or
close economic ties with such a city. All other counties—2,276 in 1993—are
nonmetropolitan. Because the county is the building block of the vast major-
ity of Federal data systems, nonmetro counties are the building blocks of
rural data systems, if only by default.

We emphasize that almost without exception, data on rural places in the
United States are based on one of these two definitions. When it comes to statistics, the designation of "rural" refers either to a place with less than 2,500

---

*Underlined numbers in parentheses refer to sources listed in the Reference section of
this book beginning on page 129.

[1]Readers interested in the status of and outlook for rural data are referred to *Rural
Information Systems: New Directions in Data Collection and Retrieval* (2).

people or to a nonmetropolitan county. Because very few Federal agencies collect data in a way that yields statistics on places with populations of less than 2,500, most of the data we use to describe "rural" places actually describes nonmetropolitan counties.

Luckily, we can speak a little more precisely about nonmetro counties by using two classification schemes developed by the USDA's Economic Research Service (ERS). The first is the Beale coding system, which classifies six groups of nonmetro counties according to how urban or rural their population is (based on the Census Bureau's definition of "rural") and whether or not they are adjacent to metropolitan areas (see box). At one end of the nonmetro spectrum are "urbanized adjacent" counties that have an urban population of at least 20,000 and are adjacent to a metro area. At the other end are "totally rural nonadjacent" counties that (1) have no urban population (that is, no place with a population of at least 2,500) and (2) are not adjacent to a metro area. (Codes for all U.S. counties are available on diskette from "ERS Data," Room 228, 1301 New York Avenue N.W., Washington, DC, 20005-4788. Call (202) 219-0534 for more information.)

The second classification scheme we can use to be more precise about nonmetro counties is the ERS County Typology system, which ERS recently revised (4). It includes six mutually exclusive economic types. Five of them—farming, mining, manufacturing, government, and services—reflect dependence on particular economic specializations. A sixth type, called "nonspecialized," includes counties not classified as having any of the five

Beale Nonmetro County Classification	Number of Counties
Urban population of 20,000 or more, and adjacent to a metro area	133
Urban population of 20,000 or more, and not adjacent to a metro area	113
Urban population of 2,500–19,999, and adjacent to a metro area	611
Urban population of 2,500–19,999, and not adjacent to a metro area	647
Completely rural (no places with a population of 2,500 or more), and adjacent to a metro area	247
Completely rural (no places with a population of 2,500 or more), and not adjacent to a metro area	525
Total nonmetro counties	2,276

Definitions used in the ERS County Typology (4)

Economic Types

Farming-dependent   Farming contributed a weighted annual average of 20 percent or more of total labor and proprietor income over the three years from 1987 to 1989. There are 556 farming-dependent counties.

Mining-dependent   Mining contributed a weighted annual average of 15 percent or more of total labor and proprietor income over the three years from 1987 to 1989. There are 146 mining-dependent counties.

Manufacturing-dependent   Manufacturing contributed a weighted annual average of 30 percent or more of total labor and proprietor income over the three years from 1987 to 1989. There are 506 manufacturing-dependent counties.

Government-dependent   Government activities contributed a weighted annual average of 25 percent or more of total labor and proprietor income over the three years from 1987 to 1989. There are 244 government-dependent counties.

Services-dependent   Service activities (private and personal services, wholesale and retail trade, finance and insurance, transportation and public utilities) contributed a weighted annual average of 50 percent or more of total labor and proprietor income over the three years from 1987 to 1989. There are 323 services-dependent counties.

Nonspecialized   Counties not classified as a specialized economic type over the three years from 1987 to 1989. There are 484 nonspecialized counties.

Policy Types

Retirement-destination   The population aged 60 years and over in 1990 increased by 15 percent or more from 1980–90 through in-migration of people. There are 190 retirement-destination counties.

Federal lands   Federally owned lands made up 30 percent or more of a county's land area in 1987. There are 270 Federal lands counties.

Commuting   Workers aged 16 years and over commuting to jobs outside their county of residence were 40 percent or more of all the county's workers in 1990. There are 381 commuting counties.

Persistent poverty   Persons with poverty-level income in the preceding year were 20 percent or more of total population in each of four years: 1960, 1970, 1980, and 1990. There are 535 persistent poverty counties.

Transfers-dependent   Income from transfer payments (Federal, state, and local) contributed a weighted annual average of 25 percent or more of total personal income over the three years from 1987 to 1989. There are 381 transfers-dependent counties.

economic specializations. The ERS County Typology scheme also identifies five overlapping, policy-relevant types: retirement-destination, Federal lands, persistent poverty, commuting, and transfers-dependent.

State tables containing the ERS county classification codes, with descriptive profiles of the different county types, are available from the ERS AutoFAX Service. (Dial (202) 219-1107 and request information directory document number 5600. See the box in Chapter 4 in the section "Agriculture" for details on using the ERS AutoFAX.) The state tables are also available via Internet–Bitnet. (E-mail Peggy J. Cook, *PROSS@ERS.BITNET,* or Karen Mizer, *KMIZER@ERS.BITNET,* for complete information.)

With these refinements to commonly used statistical reporting practices, we can at least begin to describe rural America. The centerpiece of our information base is the Census of Population and Housing that is conducted by the Department of Commerce every ten years. Using this rich data file, we can describe in detail the demographic and economic characteristics of small area populations. For example, the decennial census allows us to answer questions about work and income distribution, educational attainment, and the economic well-being of particular types of households.

In between the decennial censuses, we supplement our knowledge about rural America with a variety of less comprehensive sources. A few examples make the point. Estimates from a joint Federal–state program give us a rough idea of population change in small areas from year to year. The economic censuses that are conducted every five years permit us to describe the structure and activity of the most important industries in each county in the United States (albeit with few details). The Bureau of Economic Analysis estimates annual county-level per capita and total personal income and its components. And, data published in the *County and City Data Book* describe the health resources and status of county populations.

Who needs this kind of data? The answer is: people who analyze and make decisions about where rural communities are heading. Public and private community development practitioners, university researchers, elected officials, and policy makers from the local to the Federal level all use data and information about rural communities. The purpose of this book is to help them find what they need.

Organization of the Book

Chapter 1 describes a few basic concepts for readers who are not experienced data users. The topics discussed are: primary vs. secondary data; survey vs. administrative data; sample vs. population surveys; the media in which data are available; census geography; data mapping; and public vs. private data.

Chapter 2 provides an overview of major data sources that can be used to describe rural communities, including the Census Bureau's decennial and current population programs; the Census Bureau's agricultural, economic, and government censuses; personal income data from the Bureau of Economic Analysis; and labor market data from the Bureau of Labor Statistics. The chapter concludes by explaining where researchers can find data that are issued by these agencies, as well as where they can find more information about their state and region.

Chapters 3, 4, and 5 show how researchers can use Federal, state, and local data to understand social and economic change in the very diverse communities that make up rural America. Sample counties from the ERS County Typology groups are used to put the data sources in context. This classification scheme enables us to show how various data sources can be used to explore major rural issues, including the performance of critical economic sectors, population change, and persistent rural poverty.

The sample counties are:

- Attala County, Mississippi, a "nonspecialized," "persistent poverty," and "transfers-dependent" county;

- Coos County, New Hampshire, a "manufacturing-dependent" county;

- Kossuth County, Iowa, a "farming-dependent" county;

- Latah County, Idaho, a "government-dependent" county;

- Nicholas County, West Virginia, a "mining-dependent" and "transfers-dependent" county; and

- Yavapai County, Arizona, a "services-dependent," "retirement destination," and "Federal lands" county.

The appendices provide readers with postal and electronic addresses and phone numbers for state and Federal offices that house or collect data. They also give details about Census Bureau publications and economic census programs. A glossary at the end of the book gives definitions of research and statistical terms and, finally, a reference table on the inside back cover explains acronyms used in the text.

Several comments before we begin: First, most of this book concerns data reported by Federal agencies. However, researchers who are interested primarily in local conditions may find more up-to-date and detailed data from state and private sources (such as local employers). We also encourage people to pursue contacts in their own communities, as well as state resources (see Appendix D).

Second, knowing where to find reliable data is only one important part of research. Also critical is interpretation and analysis for decision making. To find out what kind of analysis has been done on rural communities in your state or region, contact your state land grant university, Regional Rural Development Center, or state Rural Development Council. These organizations are discussed at the end of Chapter 2.

Finally, three caveats about using the data described here: First, the value of most data lies not with a single statistic for one particular area, but in comparable statistics for different areas or different time periods. For example, an individual county's unemployment rate is more telling when compared to the rate in surrounding counties because it is put in a relative context. Our statistical indicators are too imprecise to contain "absolute truth" by themselves.

Second, statistics are only as valuable as the questions people ask. The most carefully collected data are useless if researchers have not asked questions whose answers inform us about issues that matter. To emphasize that good research begins with good questions, data in this book are described in the context of how they can be used. It is hoped that the illustrative questions we pose will encourage more substantive and useful research on rural communities.

Third, we have tried to provide accurate addresses and phone numbers for the various information contacts in this book. However, many agencies move or change phone numbers periodically. If you are unable to reach a contact with the information we provide here, please persevere by calling directory assistance or the state or regional office of the agency you are trying to contact.

1

Data Concepts

data . . . things known or assumed; facts or figures from which conclusions can be inferred; information (6)

statistics . . . facts or data of a numerical kind, assembled, classified, and tabulated so as to present significant information about a given subject (6)

Kinds of Data

Statistical data come from either primary or secondary sources. *Primary data* are those collected directly by a researcher for a specific study, using, for example, personal or telephone interviews. *Secondary sources* are existing data (collected by a government institution or private vendor) that a researcher uses for his or her particular analysis. This book is solely concerned with secondary data sources. To the extent that you find secondary sources inadequate (because of detail, accuracy, or timeliness), you may want to collect primary data. Methods to consider include conducting survey research, content analysis, or the case study technique (16).

Secondary data are collected in either survey form (by the Census Bureau, for example) or administratively in the course of an organization's normal business (by the Internal Revenue Service or Social Security Administration, for example). Both survey and administrative data are discussed in this book.

How Data Are Available

Statistical data are typically issued in one or both of two formats. The first is "hard copy," either in a publication or on a computer printout. Published data and computer printouts require no special equipment to use and are, at least for now, the most readily available. However, they are also the bulkiest and often do not contain as much detail as other formats, nor are they regularly reissued when data are revised. Furthermore, hard copy data must be manipulated or "recombined" by hand. Only occasionally do government agencies accept requests for computer printouts of specially tabulated data.

The second format in which statistical data are issued is electronic, that is, computer readable on either diskette, CD-ROM, tape, or "online." Data diskettes are available from many agencies and are commonly used for relatively small data sets. CD-ROMs are compact disks with "read-only" memory and much larger storage capacities than diskettes. They are expensive for the occasional data user and require a special computer drive to use, but they are increasingly available in libraries. Diskettes and CD-ROMs often come with utility software that makes them user friendly. In addition, more and more software is being written to meet the needs of less-specialized users.

Tapes are used only by researchers who have access to a mainframe computer and who need very large data sets. They typically require programming expertise to use.

Online data files can be accessed with a modem device, which makes it possible for computers to communicate with each other via telephone lines. Using a modem, you can read or obtain online data by connecting your personal computer to one of a variety of online commercial services, such as Prodigy or CompuServe. One example of an online database is the Census Bureau's CENDATA. It is accessible through CompuServe and DIALOG information services (see Appendix F). Even without subscribing to a commercial service, you can access some online databases on electronic bulletin

---

Public agencies make data available through the Internet . . .

The Census Bureau and many other agencies are beginning to put data online so people with personal computers and a modem no longer need bulky, hard copy reports. For example, CENDATA is the Census Bureau's online database. It gives data users access to basic information about where to go for help with Census data, as well as more detailed information, including definitions of Census geography, press releases, data from the 1990 Census of Population and Housing and the 1992 Economic Censuses, and other Census programs.

If you have access to Internet or a commercial service account, you can send electronic mail and also hook into computer sites where data and other information are stored. Giving complete instructions on how to access all the different databases that might be of interest to our readers is beyond the scope of this book. However, we have provided names, Internet addresses, and telephone numbers for agencies that provide online data (see Appendix F). Since more organizations go online all the time, we suggest that readers contact specific agencies to find out what data are available.

board services (BBS) for the cost of the phone call (long distance in most cases).

Many agencies use a hybrid of electronic technology that enables data users to access hard copies of reports via facsimile or "fax." Usually, this involves calling from the touch-tone phone on a fax machine, selecting numerical options in response to a recorded menu, and immediately (or later when you leave your fax number) receiving a hard copy by return fax.

This book focuses on data that are publicly accessible either in hard copy or electronic format, online, or in depository libraries. Researchers should contact the issuing agency if they require tape files and have the necessary hardware and expertise.

Population versus Sample Data

Each decade since 1790, the U.S. Census Bureau has conducted a population census. A *census* is a count, or enumeration, of the total population in a given area. Censuses can include things other than people. Since 1940, for example, the Census Bureau has also enumerated housing units.

Planning for the 1990 decennial census began in the early 1980s. Its total cost was roughly $2.6 billion. By mid-1990, the Bureau employed about 476,000 temporary workers in addition to its regular staff. The cost of each census has been increasing. In 1980, the cost per person was about $4, while in 1990 it was about $10. Much of the increase has been due to more extensive follow-up work to improve response rates. Now that the 1990 census population reports are all issued, data are available for areas as small as single blocks.

Contrast the decennial census with the Census Bureau's Current Population Survey (CPS), a monthly survey that gathers information from a sample of the population—about 50,000–60,000 households. A *sample* is "part" of a population carefully selected to represent the "whole" population. The Census Bureau and the Bureau of Labor Statistics (BLS) use the CPS sample to estimate many widely quoted statistics, including the national unemployment rate and the percentage of families with income below the poverty level.

The kind of data collected in the CPS is similar to that in the decennial census, but because it is comes from a sample, it cannot be used to analyze areas below the regional (and in a few cases, the state) level. Estimates about smaller geographic areas are less reliable because of the relatively small sample size.

Sampling is critical to research. By scientifically choosing a sample of observations that represents an entire population, researchers save money and time on data collection and analysis. They survey fewer people and they process fewer data.[2]

To better understand this point, consider the case of poverty estimates from the Bureau of the Census. Using only CPS sample data, the Bureau estimates the number of persons and families with incomes below the poverty level for the nation as a whole, for regions of the country (South and non-South), and for certain demographic groups (such as female-headed households in nonmetro areas). The Federal government gets the statistics it needs (and saves money) by surveying only a representative sample in between the decennial census years.

Many of the data sources described in this book are derived from samples of a population rather than from censuses. How the sample is selected, how large it is, and how much variation it contains all affect how much confidence we can have in the accuracy of sample estimates. A larger, more uniform sample yields more precise estimates, that is, a smaller sampling error. We encourage readers who use secondary, sample data to take sampling error into account; it is typically explained in the technical documentation for each data source.

Census Geography and the Notion of Rural[3]

The U.S. Census Bureau, which produces much of the data discussed in this book, reports statistics for geographical areas ranging from the entire United States to single city blocks. Some of the areas are governmental units (legally defined areas such as states and counties), while others are defined by the Census Bureau to collect and organize the data (such as census tracts and block groups). Understanding Census Bureau geography is an important part of making the most effective use of the agency's data.

Figure 1 illustrates the four census regions defined for the United States. They include the West, Midwest, Northeast, and South. Each region is composed of two or more geographic divisions or groupings of states. The states themselves consist of counties and their equivalents (3,143 plus 78 in Puerto Rico and 91 in outlying areas such as Guam and American Samoa).

---

[2]For a nontechnical discussion of sampling, see *How to Conduct Your Own Survey* (16). Note that some data collected in the decennial census are also sample-based. See Chapter 2.

[3]This discussion is abstracted from "A Guide to State and Local Census Geography" (34) and *Census Catalog and Guide: 1994* (23).

Figure 1   Census regions and geographic divisions of the United States.

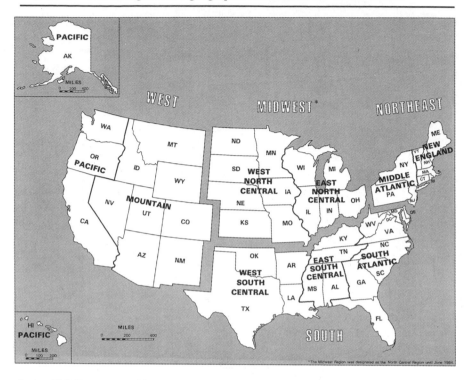

Source: U.S. Department of Commerce, Bureau of the Census (<u>34</u>).

Figure 2 shows the national geographic relationships used by the Census Bureau. Counties are divided into either (1) minor civil divisions (MCDs), which are town and township governmental units (about 30,000 total), or (2) census county divisions (CCDs). CCDs are statistical units designated by the Census Bureau in states where MCDs do not exist or are not functioning governments. They total 5,581 (plus 37 boroughs and 40 "census subareas" in Alaska, and 282 "unorganized territories" in various states).

In addition to being divided into counties (and MCDs and CCDs), states are also divided into (1) incorporated places, which are governmental designations; (2) census designated places (CDPs), which are unincorporated, closely settled population centers usually with populations of at least 1,000; and (3) consolidated cities, a special governmental unit recognized for the first time in the 1990 decennial census. Consolidated cities are units of local government in which the local incorporated government has merged with the county or MCD. Incorporated places and CDPs sometimes cross county boundaries and are therefore shown separately from the county hierarchy in Figure 2.

Figure 2 National geographic relationships.

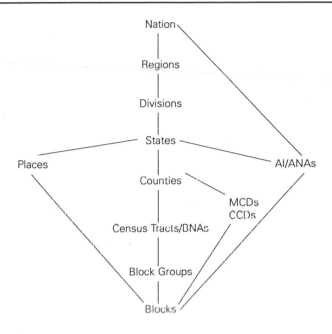

Source: U.S. Department of Commerce, Bureau of the Census (34).

In the past, MCDs and CCDs were further divided into either enumeration districts (primarily in rural areas) or block groups. Unfortunately, this system made legislative redistricting difficult for the states. Districts and block groups were too large for precise, small-area population counts, and furthermore, their boundaries did not always coincide with voting districts. To remedy these problems, the Census Bureau divided the entire United States into blocks for the 1990 Census. The definition of a *block* is a "polygon with discernable geographic features." Blocks have no minimum population. In 1990, the average block size was 70 people.

In rural areas, block boundaries may be visible features such as roads, powerlines, and shorelines. They may also include features such as fence lines, canyons, and ravines. Block-level statistics include all those data collected on the Census Bureau's "short-form" questionnaire (see Chapter 2). This information is available through all State Data Centers (see Appendix D).

Figure 3 illustrates Census Bureau small-area geography. In this scheme, the county is the largest area. It contains (1) MCDs or CCDs, and (2) census tracts or block numbering areas (BNAs). Each census tract or BNA is made up of several block groups (BGs) and consists of several individual blocks identified by a 3-digit number. For example, in Figure 3, BNA #502 has three

Figure 3   Census small-area geography.

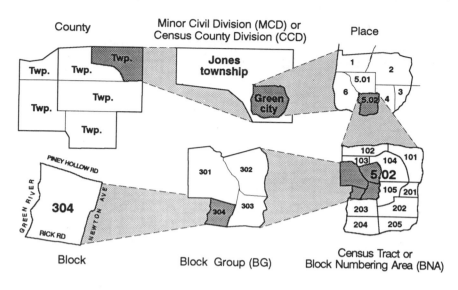

Source: U.S. Department of Commerce, Bureau of the Census (34).

block groups. The four blocks numbered 301–304 make up Block Group 3 within BNA #502.

In nonmetropolitan counties, which we discuss below, BNAs have an average population of under 4,000. Block groups average about 700 people, and blocks about 30. In more sparsely populated areas, blocks typically cover a larger geographic area; the reverse is true for more densely populated areas (36, 24).

Block-level data are only available on computer tape (Summary Tape File 1B) and laser disk (CD-ROM). Many data users like to use the CD-ROM (*1990 Census of Population and Housing Block Statistics,* CD90-1B-1). To find out where blocks are located and identify a particular location by block number, one must look at an actual Census map of the area, beginning with the county and moving to subsequently smaller geographic divisions. Depository libraries equipped to use CD-ROM usually have corresponding maps for the state. Alternatively, contact your regional Census Bureau office or State Data Center (see Appendices D and E).

The Census Bureau uses two other classification schemes that are pertinent to rural data use. As explained in the Introduction, the first scheme classifies all counties as either metropolitan or nonmetropolitan. The Office of Management and Budget (OMB) has designated some 254 metropolitan statistical areas (MSAs). In New England, MSAs consist of cities and towns, but elsewhere they are made up of one or more whole counties around a large population center, together with adjacent communities which are socially and economically integrated with the central county. Integration is measured in terms of the number of workers who commute to the central county.

An MSA must have either: (1) a city (i.e., an incorporated place) with a population of at least 50,000; or (2) an urbanized area (i.e., a Census designated area with a population of at least 50,000) and a total MSA population of at least 100,000 (75,000 in New England). For the precise definition, see "A Guide to State and Local Census Geography" (34). OMB reviews the official MSA definition each decade prior to the decennial census.

People who live in metropolitan counties comprise the metro population, while everyone else makes up the nonmetro population. In 1993, OMB classified 2,276 counties as nonmetropolitan based on 1990 census data. These counties are indicated in Figure 4.

The second scheme breaks the total population into either urban or rural. All persons living in urbanized areas (defined as central cities and surrounding densely settled territory with a combined population of at least 50,000) as well as those living in places with a population of at least 2,500 are classified

Figure 4 Nonmetro and metro counties in the United States.

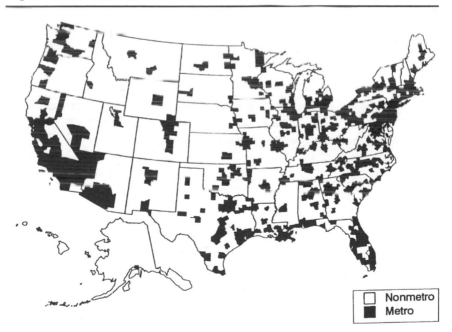

Source: U.S. Department of Agriculture, Economic Research Service, Rural Economy Division.

as urban. The rest of the population is considered rural. Further subcategories are possible, such as "rural farm/rural nonfarm" and "rural places (less than 2,500)/other rural (nonplace)."

The metro/nonmetro and urban/rural schemes are based on different concepts so they are not interchangeable, although many people confuse the two. For anyone who uses "rural" data, it is essential to understand that the Census Bureau's urban/rural split actually cuts across the metro/nonmetro split—urban areas exist within nonmetro counties and rural areas exist within metro counties.

Two useful publications on Census Bureau geography . . .

"A Guide to State and Local Census Geography" (34) includes diagrams, definitions for all Census geographic areas, and a glossary. It also profiles each state by population, land area, and the number and type of each geographic area, including American Indian and Alaska Native Areas (AI/ANAs).

"Maps and More: Your Guide to Census Bureau Geography" (36) is a brochure that defines each type of geographic area, explains small-area Census geography in detail, and tells how to read census tract and county block maps. It also lists available maps and related data products, and describes TIGER, the Census Bureau's new system for integrating data and maps.

Mapping: A New Way to Visualize Data

One of the most exciting, recent innovations in information technology is the set of tools that enables data users to show information on maps. Briefly, this technology links socioeconomic or other data to geographic coordinates. For example, it is now relatively easy to visually display on a map how poverty rates vary within a county, or how groundwater contamination is concentrated in areas with certain types of agricultural production.

To help automate mapping for the 1990 decennial census, the Census Bureau worked with the U.S. Geological Survey to develop a database of geographic and map information. The result is the TIGER database, which stands for Topologically Integrated Geographic Encoding and Referencing. The earliest version of TIGER required a large computer with a "digitizer" or device that allows the user to convert spatial measurements into digital, computer readable data. However, the 1992 TIGER files are available on CD-ROM and come with LandView, a public domain software program developed by the Environmental Protection Agency. It allows users to create maps with a personal computer and then link the maps with selected 1990 census data.

Figure 5 LandView software can be used to generate maps for small areas.

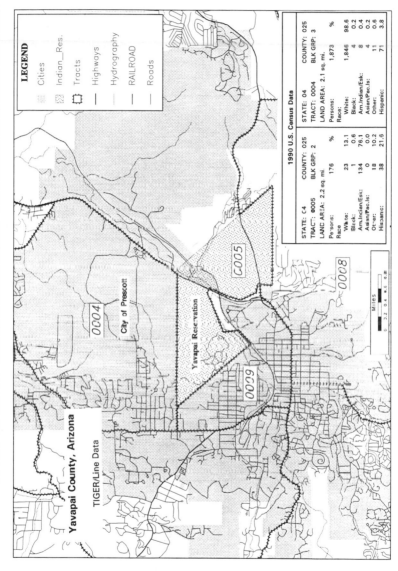

Yavapai County, Arizona

TIGER/Line Data

City of Prescott

0004

0005

Yavapai Reservation

0029

0008

Miles
0 .2 .4 .6 .8

LEGEND

- Cities
- Indian_Res.
- Tracts
- Highways
- Hydrography
- RAILROAD
- Roads

1990 U.S. Census Data

STATE: C4	COUNTY: 025
TRACT: 0005	BLK GRP: 2
LAND AREA: 2.2 sq. mi.	

Persons:	176	
Race		%
White:	23	13.1
Black:	1	0.6
Am.Incian/Esk:	134	76.1
Asian/Pac.Is:	0	0.0
Other:	18	10.2
Hispanic:	38	21.6

STATE: 04	COUNTY: 025
TRACT: 0004	BLK GRP: 3
LAND AREA: 2.1 sq. mi.	

Persons:	1,873	
Race:		%
White:	1,846	98.6
Black:	4	0.2
Am.Indian/Esk:	8	0.4
Asian/Pac.Is:	4	0.2
Other:	11	0.6
Hispanic:	71	3.8

Source: U.S. Department of Commerce, Bureau of the Census (25).

Using LandView, data users can generate a map that includes 1990 census tracts, block numbering areas (BNAs), block groups (BGs), and blocks, and displays selected, block group–level data. Depository libraries that have the new version of TIGER will also have the LandView software. Even though LandView can be used on a personal computer, loading all the data for any given geographic area, even counties, takes some time because of the large files. If you want to create a map, call your library ahead of time to let them know you are coming and to specify the geographic areas in which you are interested. You can also contact your Census Bureau regional office for help.

A word about LandView: This software is a great step toward making mapping data available to the general public. However, the Federal government is not allowed to provide software that competes with commercial vendors. Therefore, while LandView does perform basic map data retrieval and drawing functions, it is less sophisticated than other mapping or GIS (geographic information system) programs that use TIGER files. Figure 5 illustrates the kind of map that can be created for small areas, in this case, for part of Yavapai County, Arizona.

Public versus Private Data

The Census Bureau and other Federal, state, and local agencies are public data sources. The data they estimate or collect are produced at public expense in order to carry out some statutorily initiated program or regulation. These agencies make data available to the public on a cost recovery basis or free of charge, as a public service.

In contrast, private data organizations offer repackaged public data or data they collect themselves, always for a fee. There are both for-profit and non-profit private data firms. Their main customers are businesses that need easy-to-use, current statistics and forecasts to evaluate consumer markets. One private demographic firm, for example, sells a database containing current and projected population estimates by age, sex, income, education, and other characteristics for all zip codes, minor civil divisions, and counties in the United States.

As a rule, such firms are more reliable for urban areas than for rural, primarily because their business clientele are interested in larger, concentrated markets. However, some privately issued data products may suit a particular rural researcher's needs. A good place to start hunting for a suitable private data vendor is *The Insider's Guide to Demographic Know-How* by Diane Crispell, available from American Demographics Press for $49.95. American Demographics also publishes an annually updated special report called "Directory of Demographic Products and Services," which sells for $10. Call (800) 828-1133 for more information.

2

Overview of Sources

The core of our knowledge about rural issues comes from the Census of Population and Housing conducted by the Federal government every ten years. We supplement these decennial census data with other statistics from the Bureau of the Census and with information from a variety of other Federal, state, and local agencies (Figure 6).

In the sections below, we describe the most important sources of data that researchers can use to analyze rural issues. The chapter closes with a discussion of state and regional sources of rural information.

The Decennial Census of Population and Housing

The Census Bureau is the Federal agency that is primarily responsible for collecting and publishing information about individuals, households, businesses, and governments. Foremost among the agency's activities is the decennial census, which is an invaluable source of information for two reasons. First, it is exceptionally rich in the detail it provides, and second, it is nationally uniform for all geographic areas. In fact, the decennial census is our only nationally uniform, small-area source of data on such important topics as educational attainment, poverty, and occupation. It is important to understand that while local organizations, businesses, and government agencies often conduct surveys or estimate such information from secondary sources, their data cannot be compared to other areas in the country because they do not use uniform definitions and methods.

The U.S. Constitution called for the Federal government to count the population every ten years beginning in 1790. The primary reason for conducting this decennial census was to apportion or divide the number of members of the House of Representatives among the states according to their population. The second reason was to assess the nation's military and industrial strength by counting the number of males old enough to fight in the militia and work in the labor force (32).

Since 1940, the decennial census has also included the Census of Housing,

Figure 6   Major sources of data on nonmetro and rural areas.

Census of Population and Housing
(Bureau of the Census, every ten years)

Agriculture, Economic, and Government Censuses
(Bureau of the Census, every five years)

Current Population Survey and other current programs (Bureau of the Census, monthly and annual)	County Business Patterns (Bureau of the Census, annual)	County and City Data Book (Bureau of the Census, periodic)	Labor Market Information (Bureau of Labor Statistics, monthly, quarterly, annual)	Regional Economic Information System (CD-ROM) (Bureau of Economic Analysis, annual)

USA Counties
(CD-ROM)
(Bureau of the Census, annual)

Administrative and survey data from other Federal agencies, such as: • National Agricultural Statistics Service • Internal Revenue Service • Social Security Administration	Administrative and survey data from state and local agencies, such as: • Employment security • Education • Health and Welfare

which counts and collects descriptive information about the nation's occupied housing units.

In April 1990, the Bureau of the Census conducted the 21st decennial census. As in past censuses, the agency tried to survey every household in the United States. Roughly five out of every six households received a "short-form" questionnaire containing the so-called "100-percent" items, or core population and housing questions.

The remaining households, numbering roughly 17.7 million, received the "long form," which contained more detailed questions in addition to the same 100-percent items as the short form.[4] Households in rural areas were over-sampled, that is, proportionately more received the long form (1-in-2 instead of the average 1-in-6), so that small-area data could be estimated with an acceptable sampling error. Alaska Native villages and American Indian reser-

---

[4]The issue of how many households should receive the long form was hotly contested and was finally resolved in summer, 1988. The Office of Management and Budget wanted to reduce the sample rate in the interest of minimizing respondent burden. The Bureau of the Census (and others) argued that the value of the additional data outweighed respondent burden.

vations were also sampled at the higher rate to ensure a sufficient number of observations.

By law, the Census Bureau was required to deliver final population counts to the President by December 31, 1990.

> According to the Census Act of 1790, the purpose of the census was to learn the number of inhabitants in various geographic groupings, "omitting Indians not taxed, and distinguishing free persons...from all others; the sex and color of free persons; and the number of free males 16 years of age and older."

These counts are used in reapportioning representation in the U.S. Congress. By April 1, 1991, the Bureau delivered census figures accurate to the block level for purposes of state congressional redistricting. Other tabulations and publications were completed by the end of 1993 (24). (See Appendix A for a detailed list of Census reports that contain data for rural areas.)

The 1990 short form contained questions about:

Population
Name
Household relationship
Sex
Age
Marital status
Race
Hispanic origin

Housing
Number of units in structure
Number of rooms in unit
Tenure (owned or rented)
Value of home or monthly rent
Congregate housing (meals included in rent)
Vacancy characteristics

Tips on Community Research: How to Locate and Use Data

- **Find a well-informed, helpful reference librarian who can assist you in tracking down documents, phone numbers, and personal contacts.** Try your public library first, but if help is unavailable, go to the library at the nearest community college.

- **If no one in your community can help you find the data you need, call the source.** Keep calling until you get what you need. Reference books like those discussed later in this chapter are intended to help you find people to call.

- **Read the technical documentation that accompanies each of your data sources.** This material explains how the data were collected and defines terms used in the document. It may be helpful to review the questionnaire that was used to collect the data. Some agencies will make questionnaires available upon request.

- **Be precise in your use of research terms.** Make sure you understand the definitions of terms you use to describe the characteristics of your community, such as *labor force, unemployment rate,* and *poverty level.* Refer to the Glossary at the end of this book, as well as to the documentation that accompanies your data source.

The 1990 long form contained questions about:

Population	**Housing**
Social characteristics:	
Education—enrollment and attainment	Year moved into residence
	Number of bedrooms
Place of birth, citizenship, and year of entry to United States	Plumbing and kitchen facilities
	Telephone
	Autos, light trucks, and vans
Ancestry	Heating fuel, water source, and method of sewage disposal
Language spoken at home	
Migration (residence in 1985)	Year structure built
Disability	Condominium status
Fertility	Farm residence
Veteran status	Shelter costs, including utilities

Economic characteristics:
Labor force
Occupation, industry, and class of worker
Place of work and commuting to work
Work experience and income in 1989
Year last worked

Figure 7 illustrates part of a sample page from the 1990 Census of Population and Housing report, *Social and Economic Characteristics,* for Yavapai County, Arizona.

Data from the decennial and other censuses are now available on CD-ROM. Compared to the Census Bureau's printed reports, its CD-ROM files have more geographic detail but less detail on population characteristics for small areas.

Included in the Bureau's CD-ROM files is a simple retrieval program called GO that's easy to use even for people with few computer skills. Typing "GO" from the CD-ROM drive starts the program and gives a list of menu options. The user first selects a geographic area—for example, a specific county—and then chooses either summary characteristics or individual data items, such as number of households or racial characteristics. (In the case of decennial census data, summary social and economic characteristics include population numbers, education, po-

---

The Census Bureau's regional offices periodically offer training workshops on different data topics—for example, how to access data on CD-ROM. Contact your regional office for the schedule and location of training sessions (see Appendix E).

Who uses census data?

Decision makers at all levels of government and in businesses and community-based organizations use summary statistics from the decennial census. Here are some examples:

- Federal administrators use social and economic census data about communities to allocate billions of dollars worth of government programs, including Community Development Block Grants, agricultural research, cooperative extension, and Headstart.

- State transportation officials use census data about commuting patterns to plan for new highways.

- Social service agencies use census data to identify areas with high concentrations of elderly people, single parent households, and other groups that may need special assistance.

- Economic development organizations use census data about education, housing, and community infrastructure to compare conditions in local communities and identify opportunities for development.

The Census Bureau makes a special effort to help the public use their products. Customer Services staff people in the Data User Services Division (DUSD) answer questions and make referrals to specialists. DUSD also sells printed reports and data files from the Bureau's censuses and surveys. Call them at (301) 457-4100.

The symbol "(D)" is the Census Bureau's guarantee of confidentiality.

By law, the Census Bureau must keep individual responses to its questionnaires confidential. No other agency, including the Internal Revenue Service and the Immigration and Naturalization Service, has access to census records. And when the data are released to the public, they are combined in such a way that we cannot recognize any individual family or person. The same guarantee of confidentiality applies to businesses. No data are released that might permit someone to identify the operations of an individual business. The symbol "(D)" in a census report means that data have been "suppressed," that is, they have not been printed. Hence, information about individual responses is not disclosed.

Business data that are presented by industry group are frequently suppressed for rural areas and nonmetro counties. This is because the number of businesses in each industry group is so low that particular firms would be easy to spot.

Figure 7 Part of a sample page from the 1990 Census of Population *Social and Economic Characteristics* (CP90-2).

Table 154. Labor Force Characteristics by Race and Hispanic Origin: 1990—Con.

[Threshold and complementary threshold are 1,000 persons. Data based on sample and subject to sampling variability, see text. For definitions of terms and meanings of symbols, see text]

County	Yavapai County				Yuma County				
	White	American Indian, Eskimo, or Aleut	Hispanic origin (of any race)	White, not of Hispanic origin	White	Black	American Indian, Eskimo, or Aleut	Asian or Pacific Islander	Hispanic origin (of any race)
LABOR FORCE STATUS									
Persons 16 years and over	**83 980**	**1 239**	**4 688**	**80 789**	**61 667**	**2 084**	**1 104**	**974**	**28 759**
In labor force	41 238	612	2 773	39 379	34 961	1 566	649	682	17 660
Percent of persons 16 years and over	49.1	49.4	59.2	48.7	56.7	75.1	58.8	70.0	61.4
Armed Forces	37	2	—	37	3 503	552	36	115	503
Civilian labor force	41 201	610	2 773	39 342	31 458	1 014	613	567	17 157
Employed	38 702	545	2 526	37 003	28 382	929	514	491	13 949
At work 35 or more hours	27 648	375	1 819	26 395	22 374	692	416	368	10 409
Unemployed	2 499	65	247	2 339	3 076	85	99	76	3 208
Percent of civilian labor force	6.1	10.7	8.9	5.9	9.8	8.4	16.2	13.4	18.7
Not in labor force	42 742	627	1 915	41 410	26 706	518	455	292	11 099
Institutionalized persons	1 087	72	47	1 040	763	82	6	7	380
Females 16 years and over	**43 607**	**654**	**2 382**	**41 920**	**30 309**	**734**	**559**	**522**	**14 400**
In labor force	18 623	305	1 185	17 786	13 902	514	275	290	6 895
Percent of females 16 years and over	42.7	46.6	49.7	42.4	45.9	70.0	49.2	55.6	47.9
Armed Forces	9	2	—	9	246	29	—	5	69
Civilian labor force	18 614	303	1 185	17 777	13 656	485	275	285	6 826
Employed	17 414	285	1 028	16 682	12 132	438	244	226	5 289
At work 35 or more hours	10 702	168	652	10 236	8 484	328	187	159	3 247
Unemployed	1 200	18	157	1 095	1 524	47	31	59	1 537
Percent of civilian labor force	6.4	5.9	13.2	6.2	11.2	9.7	11.3	20.7	22.5
Not in labor force	24 984	349	1 197	24 134	16 407	220	284	232	7 505
Institutionalized persons	612	—	18	594	255	9	—	—	40
Males 16 to 19 years	**2 611**	**71**	**238**	**2 460**	**2 477**	**132**	**78**	**26**	**1 899**
Employed	1 084	30	72	1 047	921	33	27	—	530
Unemployed	255	—	11	244	180	17	—	4	198
Not in labor force	1 266	41	155	163	1 247	45	46	22	1 131

How to read data in a Census Bureau report . . .

Figure 7 illustrates part of a typical table produced by the Census Bureau. In the Arizona volume of *Social and Economic Characteristics,* Table 154 covers seven pages and includes data for each of the state's 15 counties. The purpose of Table 154 is to report data on the labor force characteristics of people in different racial groups and those who are of Hispanic origin.

The first line of data, "Persons 16 years and over," includes all people who are at least 16 years of age in each racial and Hispanic origin group. In Yavapai County, for example, there are 83,980 white persons 16 years and over, 1,239 American Indians, Eskimos, or Aleuts, and so on. Note that since racial and Hispanic groups under a certain size are not included in this table, there is no total column. Hence, we cannot find out the total number of persons 16 years of age and older from Table 154. However, by checking the Table Finding Guide at the beginning of the volume, we learn that data on the total labor force is reported in Table 144.

The 12th line in Table 154 covers females who are at least 16 years or older. Researchers who want to know the labor force characteristics of males 16 years and over by race and Hispanic origin need to subtract line 12 (females) from line 1 (all).

Row labels are indented (or reverse indented) to indicate subgroups and percentages. For example, line 1 includes all people 16 years and over, line 2 (reverse indented) includes only people 16 years and over who are in the labor force, and line 3 (indented further) shows the percentage of people 16 years and over who are in the labor force (line 2 divided by line 1). Line 10 includes persons age 16 years and over who are not in the labor force. Hence, line 2 plus line 10 (not in labor force) equals line 1.

Note that terms used in the table, such as "civilian labor force," are defined in the report appendices. Check the definitions before using the data to describe the characteristics of your community.

---

verty status, housing, and labor force statistics.) A table with the selected data is then displayed on the screen and can also be printed or downloaded to a diskette. Some libraries are also equipped to use EXTRACT, a more complicated Census Bureau program that allows users to read data for more than one geographic area at a time (for example, the number of families below the poverty level for two or more counties). Some libraries also have more sophisticated, commercial software programs that can be used with CD-ROM files.

"Census, CD-ROM and You! New Horizons for Microcomputer Users of Census Bureau Data" is a booklet that gives an overview of data available on CD-ROM and the software that can be used to read and manipulate the data. Single copies are free. Order from Customer Services at (301) 457-4100.

Current Population Reports and Surveys

The Census Bureau also collects demographic information in between the decennial censuses, so-called "intercensal" information. Under a contract with the Bureau of Labor Statistics, the agency conducts the Current Population Survey (CPS) for which they interview a sample of between 50,000 and 60,000 households every month. CPS data are the basis for estimates on employment, unemployment, poverty, income, education, and many other population characteristics.

Because CPS data are from a relatively small sample, they are not available below the regional level (except for some of the larger states). However, they are useful for tracking national and regional (South and non-South) trends between the decennial censuses. Some reports, for example, "Income, Poverty, and Valuation of Noncash Benefits: 1993," also make metro/non-metro breaks in the data and therefore give us a bird's-eye view of conditions within the nonmetro population.

For more up-to-date information about population change and per capita money income in counties and subcounty areas, the Census Bureau cooperates with state agencies under the Federal–State Cooperative Program for Population Estimates. In addition, many states make their own estimates about more detailed characteristics of local populations, such as age, race, and ethnicity. These annual statistics enable researchers to answer questions about how the composition of the local population is changing.

Other Censuses

In addition to the decennial census of population and housing, the Census Bureau conducts national agriculture, economic, and government censuses twice each decade in the years ending in "2" and "7." Most of these censuses yield data for counties, and in some cases, for subcounty areas.

Reports from the 1992 censuses are being released as this book goes to press. Those in the 1992 series that have the title "Geographic Area Series" typically contain the most small-area data (see Appendix B).

Unlike the population census, which uses the household as its unit of observation, the agriculture and economic censuses survey establishments. The Census Bureau defines an *establishment* as a "business or industrial unit at a single physical location that produces or distributes goods or performs services" (39). Establishment lists are compiled from a variety of administrative sources and are updated continually.

For its census of agriculture, the Census Bureau tries to survey the operator of every establishment in the United States which had (or potentially had) at least $1,000 of agricultural product sales in the preceding year. The agri-

The Standard Industrial Classification, or SIC, system is a standard scheme for grouping establishments by the type of economic activity in which they are primarily engaged. Researchers in and out of government use this system because it is so comprehensive—virtually all establishments can be classified.

The SIC system is hierarchical, which means it goes from very general to very specific. Its broadest level has ten divisions: agriculture, forestry, and fishing; mining; construction; manufacturing; transportation, communications, electric, gas, and sanitary services; wholesale trade; retail trade; finance, insurance, and real estate; services; and public administration.

Each division is subdivided into "2-digit" major groups, "3-digit" industry groups, and "4-digit" industries. For example, "Services" (SIC 70-89) is one of the ten divisions. A subdivision within Services includes:

SIC Level	Example
Major industry group 72	Personal services
Industry group 721	Laundry, cleaning, garments
Industry 7211	Power laundries, family and commercial

Another major industry group in the Services Division is Social Services, SIC 83. Advocacy groups, community development organizations, and regional planning agencies are grouped in "Social Services, Not Elsewhere Classified," SIC 8399.

The Census Bureau and other agencies publish data about establishments at the most detailed SIC level possible without disclosing confidential information.

The most recent edition of the Standard Industrial Classification Manual was published in 1987. It is available in many public libraries and is for sale by the National Technical Information Service (NTIS).

cultural census yields county-level (as well as state- and national-level) data on number and type of farms, land in farms, operator characteristics, value of agricultural sales, selected operating expenses, and other characteristics. The 1992 Census of Agriculture, published on a state-by-state basis, was released in 1994.

For its economic censuses, the Census Bureau organizes establishment data by geographic area and type of economic activity or Standard Industrial Classification (SIC), a system which has been defined by the Office of Management and Budget. Since the Census Bureau cannot disclose information about individual establishments, fewer statistics are available for small areas. Appendix B shows the types of economic data that are available at the county level.

Economists use data from the economic censuses and other sources to estimate the gross domestic product (GDP), productivity, and other measures of economic activity. Researchers can use the data to find out, for example, how various industries contribute to the local economy in terms of payroll, the purchase of supplies and other inputs, and the value of products and services sold outside the area.

The Census of Governments is conducted every five years and is supplemented by annual and quarterly surveys. Unlike the economic censuses, the government censuses are not covered by the disclosure limitation that suppresses information about individual observations. Thus, the level of detail in the government census reports is greater.

Data on revenue sources, expenditures, tax bases, and employment are available for roughly 85,000 units of local government including counties, municipalities, townships, school districts, and special districts. Private firms that sell products or services to local governments use these data to identify marketing opportunities. Community researchers can use them to understand how their local government is structured and how various government units generate revenue and spend money.

Other Surveys from the Census Bureau

The Census Bureau's economic activities also include several surveys—for example, the Annual Survey of Manufacturers and the Survey of Minority-Owned Business Enterprises. In general, these surveys yield little or no small-area data. The exception is *County Business Patterns* (*CBP*), which is issued annually and is based on data from establishment surveys and administrative records. *CBP* presents national-, state-, and county-level business data by 2-, 3-, and 4-digit SIC codes. *CBP* can be used to answer questions about the number of employees and firms in particular industries. Because it is published annually, researchers can keep track of year-to-year changes in the structure of local economies. Figure 8 illustrates part of a sample page from *CBP* for Nicholas County, West Virginia.

Other Economic Data

The Bureau of Economic Analysis (BEA) is another agency in the U.S. Department of Commerce that makes economic estimates that are useful for describing nonmetropolitan (and other) counties. Unlike the Census Bureau, BEA does not conduct surveys or censuses itself, but uses administrative and survey information collected by others to make its estimates of personal income (by type and industry) and employment.

Each year, BEA releases a CD-ROM, *Regional Economic Information System* (*REIS*), which contains county-level personal income data from 1969

Figure 8 Part of a sample page from *County Business Patterns*

Table 2. Counties—Employees, Payroll, and Establishments, by Industry: 1992—Con.

[Excludes most government employees, railroad employees, and self-employed persons. Size class 1 to 4 includes establishments having payroll but no employees during mid-March pay period. For explanation of terms, statement on reliability, and comparability with other data, see introductory text.] (D) denotes figures withheld to avoid disclosing data for individual companies.

SIC code	Industry	Number of employees for week including March 12	Payroll ($1,000) First quarter	Payroll ($1,000) Annual	Total number of establishments	Number of establishments by employment-size class 1 to 4	5 to 9	10 to 19	20 to 49	50 to 99	100 to 249	250 to 499	500 to 999	1,000 or more
	NICHOLAS													
	Total ----------	5 977	29 937	124 321	632	348	146	72	48	10	8	-	-	-
	Agricultural services, forestry, and fishing ---	30	40	481	8	6	2	-	-	-	-	-	-	-
12	Mining ----------	1 394	14 513	54 329	50	11	7	10	15	3	4	-	-	-
	Coal mining ----------	1 374	14 285	53 339	45	8	6	9	15	3	4	-	-	-
122	Bituminous coal and lignite mining ------	1 080	11 771	45 611	35	6	4	7	12	3	3			
1221	Bituminous coal and lignite surface ------	440	5 330	21 848	11	-	4	6	2	2	1			
1222	Bituminous coal underground ------	603	5 969	22 894	19	3	4	-	9	1	2			
124	Coal mining services ------	208	1 900	6 271	7	1	2	2	1	-	1			
15	Construction ----------	200	624	4 722	46	33	9	3	-	1	-			
151	General contractors and operative builders ------	102	408	3 416	24	14	7	3	-	-	-			
	General building contractors ------	87	372	3 251	18	9	6	3	-	-	1			
16	Heavy construction, except building ------	(B)	(D)	(D)	4	3	-	-	-	-	1			
162	Heavy construction, except highway ------	(B)	(C)	(D)	3	2	-	-	-	-	1			

to the most current year available (see box on page 56 for more information). These CD-ROM files replace the annual printed report, *Local Area Personal Income*. *LAPI* will continue to be published once every five years, most recently in 1994. It will contain data from 1969 to the most recent reference year, so it will be a good source of historical information. However, it will only include three statistics for each county: population, per capita personal income, and total personal income. Figure 9 illustrates part of a sample page from *LAPI* for Latah County, Idaho.

BEA county income data are widely used to analyze the industrial structure of local economies and to evaluate the impact of various public and private programs. Researchers can use BEA data to find out how total and per capita income is changing in their county, and to what extent local residents depend on different sources of income (for example, wages and salaries, retirement payments, and interest and dividend income).

BEA makes its personal income and other data accessible to local users through its Regional Economic Information System (REIS) and the BEA User Groups. REIS includes data files, computer programs, and staff responsible for the regional BEA databases. REIS responds to specific data requests and also distributes BEA data at no cost to over 200 members of the BEA User Groups around the country. Members of the User Groups (typically located in government agencies and universities) distribute data free of charge or at minimal cost within their own state. Researchers can locate BEA User Groups in their state by calling REIS at (202) 606-5360.

BEA also publishes a monthly report called *Survey of Current Business*. The April issue of the *Survey* includes annual personal income data by county and current business statistics, including consumer and producer price indexes.

BEA has a fax-based service that allows customers to access news releases and other information 24 hours a day. Information is available on regional economic trends and includes some county-level data. Dial 1-900-786-2329 from a fax machine's touch-tone telephone and respond to the recorded instructions. Each call costs $0.65 per minute.

For more information on BEA's information services, order the free publication "A User's Guide to BEA Information" from Public Information Office, Order Desk BE-53, BEA, 1441 L St. NW, U.S. Department of Commerce, Washington, DC 20230 or call (202) 606-9900. BEA also publishes a free list of telephone contacts for data users.

Another important source of economic information about rural communities is the Economic Research Service (ERS) in the U.S. Department of Agriculture. Using data primarily collected by other agencies, ERS carries out research on the production and marketing of major farm commodities; foreign agriculture and trade; economic use, conservation, and development of natural resources; trends in rural population, employment, and housing;

Figure 9 Part of a sample page from *Local Area Personal Income 1969–1992.*

Latah County

	1969	1970	1971	1972	1973	1974	1975	1976	1977	1978	1979	1980
Total personal income (thousands of dollars)	68,102	74,385	82,425	94,012	112,298	137,284	133,260	151,212	158,325	186,1□□	205,657	231,465
Total population (thousands)	24.4	25.1	26.3	27.5	27.5	27.7	27.4	27.6	27.8	2□□	28.3	28.9
Per capita personal income (dollars)	2,790	2,988	3,130	3,418	4,078	4,957	4,870	5,483	5,692	6,6□□	7,278	8,015

	1981	1982	1983	1984	1985	1986	1987	1988	1989	1990	1991	1992
Total personal income (thousands of dollars)	248,246	246,154	272,143	287,880	303,433	323,784	333,920	356,624	404,281	433,0□5	451,966	487,546
Total population (thousands)	29.2	30.0	30.2	30.2	30.6	30.0	30.1	29.9	30.2	3□.6	31.1	31.8
Per capita personal income (dollars)	8,491	8,217	9,017	9,545	9,900	10,793	11,090	11,914	13,377	14,□□4	14,527	15,347

Lemhi County

	1969	1970	1971	1972	1973	1974	1975	1976	1977	1978	1979	1980
Total personal income (thousands of dollars)	14,864	16,537	18,295	21,344	24,774	26,238	28,209	33,554	37,279	41,□52	49,979	57,779
Total population (thousands)	5.5	5.6	5.7	6.1	6.3	5.4	6.4	6.5	6.7	7.0	7.3	7.5
Per capita personal income (dollars)	2,688	2,949	3,190	3,505	3,961	4,118	4,392	5,167	5,540	5,□94	6,858	7,664

	1981	1982	1983	1984	1985	1986	1987	1988	1989	1990	1991	1992
Total personal income (thousands of dollars)	60,644	62,709	64,659	65,958	67,165	69,098	71,978	76,962	83,857	89,□86	92,910	99,067
Total population (thousands)	7.9	8.0	8.0	3.0	7.5	6.9	6.9	7.0	6.9	6.9	7.0	7.1
Per capita personal income (dollars)	7,717	7,802	8,055	8,289	8,913	9,977	10,430	11,067	12,153	12,□89	13,216	13,993

The Rural Economy Division (RED) of ERS is the largest Federal agency devoted entirely to research on rural issues. RED economists, sociologists, demographers, political scientists, and geographers analyze national and regional trends affecting rural communities. Their research is intended to inform policy makers and program managers at all levels of the public and private sectors.

Each of RED's four branches focuses on a unique aspect of rural America. For more information, call the branch chief whose phone number is listed below.

- The *Population, Labor, and Income Branch* monitors indicators of rural well-being, including farm household income, rural poverty, and the rural workforce (202) 219-0533.

- The *Rural Industry Branch* studies industrial structure as well as the links between rural economies and larger national and international economies (202) 219-0527.

- The *Farm Business Economics Branch* collects and disseminates current information and future projections on the economic health of the farm sector and is the central data collection program for ERS research (202) 219-0001.

- The *Finance and Development Branch* studies the effects of key services and resources on the economic development of rural communities, and is especially concerned with the effects of Federal policies on rural communities (202) 219-0721.

RED publishes a magazine called *Rural Development Perspectives,* that presents results and implications of new research by ERS and other analysts. A one-year subscription (three issues) costs $14. The agency also publishes *Rural Conditions and Trends,* a periodical about rural and national economic trends. For example, the Spring 1994 issue included articles on national economic growth; rural employment growth; rural household income; and rural poverty and population. An annual subscription (2 issues) costs $13. Both publications can be ordered from ERS/NASS, 341 Victory Drive, Herndon, VA 22070, (800) 999-6779.

rural economic adjustment problems; and performance of the U.S. agricultural industry. Although most ERS reports and analyses address regional and national issues, the agency's broad expertise makes it an invaluable and unique resource for those concerned with rural communities.

Reports is a periodic ERS catalog that lists all current agency research reports and other publications. To be placed on the free mailing list for *Reports,* contact the ERS's Information Division, Room 237, 1301 New York Ave. NW, Washington, DC 20005-4789 or call (800) 999-6779. The Information Division also issues a free diskette that contains a "Finder's Advisory System." The DOS-formatted diskette includes a complete listing of ERS data products, information specialists, and publications. No programming knowledge is required to use the system and free updates are sent on request. To order, contact Jim Horsfield at Room 724, 1301 New York Ave. NW, Washington, DC 20005-4788, call (202) 219-0698, or e-mail (*JIMH@ERS.BITNET*).

Labor Market Information

Another important source of information about rural communities is the Bureau of Labor Statistics (BLS), which is the Federal government's principal data gathering agency on the subject of labor economics. BLS surveys businesses, works with the Census Bureau on the Current Population Survey, and cooperates with state agencies to produce a wealth of labor force statistics. Using BLS annual, quarterly, and monthly data, economists and other analysts can track the level of economic activity in the country as a whole and in specific regions; gauge the health of individual industries; and compare wage rates and earnings among specific demographic groups. Using annual county-level estimates prepared by BLS and individual states, researchers can learn how many people are working in various industries, how much they earn, and (on a monthly basis) how many people are unemployed.

Two BLS programs yield small-area data—Employment, Wages, and Contributions (ES-202) and Local Area Unemployment Statistics. For more information on BLS, see *Major Programs of the Bureau of Labor Statistics* (46) or call Information Services at (202) 606-7828. BLS provides a free list of telephone contacts for data users and also makes press releases and time series data available on Internet (see Appendix F). Non-Internet users can access limited information by dialing directly into an electronic bulletin board service for the price of the call at (202) 606-7060.

Where to Find Data Products

Data products issued by the Federal government (including reports, computer-accessible files, microfiche, and maps) are available at various locations in every state. Most accessible are the 1,300 public libraries that belong to the Federal depository library program. These libraries receive selected Federal publications that their staff believes will be useful to local patrons. Appendix D lists one Federal depository library for each state and the District of Columbia.

An additional 120 public libraries are designated as Census depository libraries. Their function is to ensure that Census Bureau publications are widely available to the public. To find the depository library closest to you, call the library listed for your state in Appendix D or Data User Services Division at the Census Bureau, (301) 457-4100. See the beginning of this chapter for tips on what to do if your local library does not have what you need.

Other sources of Federal data products are agencies belonging to the State Data Center (SDC) program, which has offices in all states, the District of Columbia, Guam, Puerto Rico, and the Virgin Islands. This program typically includes a state executive or planning office as the lead agency, a major state university and/or state library, and a network of affiliates throughout the state. The Census Bureau provides the lead agencies with Census products and training. In return, the SDCs are responsible for disseminating Census products free of charge or at low cost to data users throughout the state. The services offered by individual SDCs vary according to local leadership and funding. A list of SDC lead agencies is included in Appendix D.

Two government agencies sell data products on a cost recovery basis. These products include hard copy, microfiche, and computer readable reports. The agencies are: (1) the Government Printing Office (GPO), Superintendent of Documents, P.O. Box 371954, Pittsburgh, PA 15250-7954, (202) 512-1800, and its branches around the country; and (2) the National Technical Information Service (NTIS), 5285 Port Royal Road, Springfield, VA 22161, (703) 487-4763. GPO generally sells printed reports, while NTIS sells electronic data products and typically distributes more technical reports. NTIS is also responsible for making some government data files available to the public. More historic data may also be available from the Center for Electronic Records, National Archives and Records Administration, 8601 Adelphi Road, College Park, MD 20740, (303) 713-6630.

The Freedom of Information Act

Not all of the data collected by the Federal government are made available to the public as a matter of course. For example, administrative data collected in the process of running various public programs are not routinely published or issued in any other form. Even so, these data are very often available through the Freedom of Information Act (FOIA). This law gives any person the right to request and receive documents, files, and other records from any Federal agency, subject to certain restrictions (such as national security).

To make a FOIA request, it is important to know specifically what information you want and which agency has it. The process is relatively simple, and while requests are sometimes denied, they can be appealed. For sample request letters and more information, either contact the Freedom of Information Clearinghouse, P.O. Box 19367, Washington, DC 20036, (202) 833-3000, or see "A Citizen's Guide on Using the Freedom of Information Act and the Privacy Act of 1974 to Request Government Records," U.S. Government Printing Office, Washington, DC, 1993.

Useful Reference Materials and Statistical Compendia

The Census Bureau produces four reference publications to inform data users about its activities and reports. The most comprehensive reference publication is the annual *Census Catalog and Guide,* which provides a product overview and index, abstracts of all recent products, ordering information and forms, and sources of assistance. The catalog can be purchased for $22 from the Government Printing Office in Washington, DC, and is also available in many libraries.

The "Monthly Product Announcement" updates references cited in the catalog and is available at no cost from the Bureau's Customer Services Division at (301) 763-4100, or online through CENDATA.

"Census and You" is a monthly newsletter about new products and issues of interest to data users. For example, the June 1994 issue included articles about the growth of AIDS in Sub-Saharan Africa; the number and characteristics of "latch key" children; recently published Census reports on Federal expenditures by states and communities; and the demographic characteristics of people with professional degrees. A one-year subscription to "Census and You" can be purchased from the Government Printing Office for $21. Parts of this report are also available online through CENDATA.

"Census '90 Basics" is one booklet in the Bureau's 1990 CPH-I series of publications on products from the decennial census. It describes the design and content of the 1990 census. It also discusses Census geography and data products, and lists major printed reports by title, content, and geographic areas. "Census '90 Basics" is free from Customer Services at the Census Bureau.

"Factfinder for the Nation" is an occasional series of pamphlets that describe the range of Census materials available on topics such as population, housing, and foreign trade. Factfinder Number 22, issued in October 1991, describes data available for small areas, including counties, cities, and county subdivisions (31). Issues in the series are available from Customer Services at the Census Bureau for a nominal charge. (See the *Census Catalog and Guide* for a complete listing.)

The *County and City Data Book* (*CCDB*) is an invaluable compendium of socioeconomic data from the most recent censuses of population and housing, government, and agriculture; economic censuses; and other sources. Although it gives little historical data, the *CCDB* is useful because it provides such a wide range of data for small areas. Data are presented for counties, incorporated cities with 25,000 or more, and incorporated places and MCDs with 2,500 or more. The *CCDB* is issued periodically. The most recent editions were published in 1983, 1988, and 1994.

The 1994 *CCDB* presents over 200 data items for counties, including:

- Area (1990), population (1992), and percent population change (1980–1992);

- Population characteristics (1990);

- Number and size of households (1990);

- Vital statistics (1988) and health care (1990 and 1991);

- Hospital beds (1991), social welfare programs (1990), and crime (1991);

- Education levels (1990);

- Money income (1989);

- Housing (1990) and building permits (1992);

- Civilian labor force (1991) and employment by industry (1990);

- Personal income (1990) and farm earnings (1990);

- Agriculture (1987), manufacturing (1987), wholesale trade (1987), retail trade (1987), taxable service industries (1987);

- Banking (1992), Federal funds and grants (1992), and local government finances (1986–1987);

- Government employment (1990) and elections (1992).

Part of a sample page from the county table in the *CCDB* is shown in Figure 10.

Roughly two-thirds of the items listed above are also presented for cities with a population of 25,000 or more, and three items are presented for places with populations 2,500 and above (1990 population, 1989 per capita money income, and 1989 median household income).

The most recent *CCDB* is available on CD-ROM and diskette, as well as in published format. The printed version is available from the Government Printing Office for $40. Call Census Bureau Customer Services for the latest ordering information at (202) 457-4100.

USA Counties is a statistical abstract supplement issued only on CD-ROM. Updated annually, it provides time-series data for counties from the 1970 to 1990 Censuses of Population and Housing; Economic Census data from 1972, 1977, 1982, and 1987; and over 2,500 data items for each county in the United States. User notes provide information about changes in methodology that affect the results of time-series analysis.

Information U.S.A. is a private company that publishes helpful reference materials for researchers. *Lesko's Info–Power* (formerly *Information U.S.A.*) is a catalog of information resources in the Federal government. Although

Figure 10   Part of a sample page from the *County and City Data Book*.

Table B. Counties — **Area and Population**

Metropolitan area code[1]	State and county code[2]	County	Land area,[3] 1990 (Sq. mi.)	1992 Total persons	1992 Rank[4]	1992 Per square mile[5]	Population 1990	Population 1980	Net change, 1980–1992 Number	Net change, 1980–1992 Percent	Race White	Race Black	Race American Indian, Eskimo, or Aleut	Race Asian or Pacific Islander
			1	2	3	4	5	6	7	8	9	10	11	12
	28 000	MISSISSIPPI	46 914	2 615 203	X	56	2 573 216	2 520 770	94 438	3.7	1 633 461	91 057	8 525	13 016
...	28 001	Adams	460	34 749	1 156	75	35 356	38 07?	-3 322	-8.7	18 028	212	40	63
...	28 003	Alcorn	400	32 560	1 218	81	3? 722	33 036	-476	-1.4	28 085	540	22	53
...	28 005	Amite	730	13 408	2 115	18	13 328	13 369	39	.3	7 272	038	11	6
...	28 007	Attala	735	18 382	1 780	25	18 481	19 365	-1 483	-7.5	11 114	299	32	28
...	28 009	Benton	407	7 967	2 579	20	8 046	8 153	-186	-2.3	4 869	168	5	4
...	28 011	Bolivar	876	41 827	981	48	41 875	45 965	-4 138	-9.0	15 259	326	26	138
...	28 013	Calhoun	587	14 844	2 020	25	14 908	15 664	-820	-5.2	10 829	027	12	4
...	28 015	Carroll	528	9 304	2 449	15	9 237	9 776	-472	-4.8	5 560	654	11	10
...	28 017	Chickasaw	502	18 004	1 800	36	18 085	17 851	153	.9	11 060	981	21	19
...	28 019	Choctaw	419	9 031	2 468	22	9 071	8 995	35	.4	6 319	731	9	10
...	28 021	Claiborne	487	11 545	2 261	24	11 370	12 279	-734	-6.0	1 994	340	20	16
...	28 023	Clarke	691	17 321	1 849	25	17 313	16 945	376	2.2	11 312	977	6	8
...	28 025	Clay	409	21 387	1 625	52	21 120	21 082	305	1.4	9 789	266	19	32
...	28 027	Coahoma	554	31 628	1 252	57	31 665	36 918	-5 290	-14.3	11 001	454	20	112
...	28 029	Copiah	777	27 831	1 387	36	27 592	26 503	1 328	5.0	13 602	920	21	27

some of the material in the book is out of date, it is still a valuable guide to agencies and experts. The company also publishes *The Federal Database Finder* (revised edition due out in 1995). Check your local library or contact Information U.S.A., P.O. Box E, Kensington, MD 20895, (301) 924-0556.

Congressional Information Service (CIS), another private firm, publishes many useful indexes to reports from the Federal government and from states, municipalities, and private companies. The *American Statistics Index* (*ASI*), for example, enables researchers to find statistics produced by Federal agencies. *ASI* classifies statistics by subject, type of data breakdown (for example, metro/nonmetro), and publication title. Many college and university libraries have the *ASI*, and it is also available on CD-ROM and online through DIALOG. The *Statistical Reference Index* (*SRI*) classifies statistics that have been published by state agencies, universities, and private sector organizations. *SRI* is also available in published format or CD-ROM (but not online). For a free catalog of CIS products, write CIS, Inc., 4520 East–West Highway, Suite 800, Bethesda, MD 20814-3389, or call (800) 638-8380.

Local and Regional Information

Finding secondary data is not the only part of researching rural issues. Often, researchers need to learn what analysis has already been conducted on their community and region. A good place to start is at one of the four Regional Rural Development Centers, located in Oregon, Iowa, Mississippi, and Pennsylvania. The centers disseminate and sometimes elaborate on research conducted by land grant universities. Each one has a newsletter that profiles recent work and available resources. For a combined report of the centers' publications and projects, contact any one of the regional offices listed in Appendix C.

In addition to the four centers, another useful contact for analysis of rural issues is the Rural Information Center (RIC) at the National Agricultural Library (NAL) in Beltsville, Maryland. The RIC provides information and

---

A little research from RIC goes a long way . . .

In 1990 a mine in New Mexico was about to close. Working with a regional development organization, the mining company asked the Rural Information Center to help it find markets for zeolite, a mineral it could produce in great quantity. RIC staff performed a literature search that yielded new information on the uses of zeolite. As a result, the company identifed six new markets, kept twelve existing jobs, hired enough new employees to staff double shifts, and significantly increased plant wages. (Information provided by USDA staff and from 21.)

referral services to local officials, community development professionals, and private citizens. The staff can answer questions on topics such as current USDA research, Cooperative Extension Service programs, and economic development funding sources. They also conduct database searches and help people use the NAL collection. You can contact the RIC through your county or state extension office, by telephone at (800) 633-7701, or by mail at NAL, RIC, Room 304, 10301 Baltimore Blvd., Beltsville, MD 20705-2351.

The NAL also operates the Agricultural Library Forum (ALF), an electronic bulletin board that provides access to RIC publications and other rural development information. See Appendix F for access information.

Finally, other good contacts for rural information are the Rural Development Councils that have been established in most of the fifty states. Together with a National Council, these state councils make up the National Rural Development Partnership (NRDP), established to coordinate existing resources and support collective action between public and private organizations. The state councils are intended to bring together Federal, state, tribal, and local governments, and the private sector (profit, nonprofit, and community-based organizations) to identify and remove barriers to rural development. The national and state councils work together to link resources that can be applied in more than one rural area or state.

For more information, write the NRDP at 300 7th Street SW, Suite 714, Washington, DC 20024-4703, or call (202) 690-2394. A list of state councils and information about the program can be accessed on Internet through gopher (RURDEV.USDA.GOV).

Summary

The Census Bureau, Bureau of Economic Analysis, Bureau of Labor Statistics, and Economic Research Service provide researchers with a core of rural information that can be supplemented by the land grant universities, Regional Rural Development Centers, Rural Information Center, and State Rural Development Councils. The next three chapters illustrate how researchers can use data from these and other, more-specialized sources to understand local population and community resources, economies, and governments.

3

Characterizing Local Population and Community Resources

During the 1980s, net migration in nonmetro counties was negative—almost one million more people moved away from nonmetro counties than moved into them. Between 1990 and 1992, however, the trend was reversed—almost 400,000 more people moved into nonmetro counties than moved away from them.

These net migration figures are the aggregate numbers on which demographers and other analysts base estimates about overall trends in rural America. The problem with numbers like these is that they hide the great diversity of rural places. Like the very word *rural,* they imply that there is one kind of rural community in America, undifferentiated by size, location, or economic base. Too often, aggregate numbers prevent us from viewing social and economic organization along a set of continuums—from the suburbs of densely populated urban areas to remote, sparsely settled regions; from diversified small cities to single-industry towns; from persistent poverty to newly acquired wealth. The word *rural* has been used to embody all these extremes and many places in between.

As readers of this book probably understand firsthand, local, small-area statistics are critical to discovering new opportunities for development. Only by knowing the specific circumstances and characteristics of a particular place can community leaders map a future within the national and international context. More specifically, leaders at the local level need to know the characteristics of community residents, such as the population size and its age structure. To strengthen and diversify their local economy, leaders need to understand their community's resources, such as educational and other labor force characteristics, and distribution of income. This chapter explains how researchers can find information like this using data from the Census Bureau and other Federal and state sources.

The General Population

Demography—or the science of population—is concerned with the size, geographic distribution, composition, and change of human populations (18). Demographic change in a particular community depends on the population's characteristics (for example, the number and age of local residents) as well as on broader social and economic trends in the nation as a whole (such as increased female labor force participation or improved standards of living).

Demographic change affects the local economy by shifting the demand for goods and services. For example, if the number of families with young children increases, the community may need more day-care facilities, classroom space, and teachers. Conversely, if the number of elderly people grows, the community may need specialized transportation, more geriatric care, and a new nursing home. Community leaders need to understand these changes so they can plan for future development.

The broad question that should be asked is: what is happening to the size and characteristics of the local population and why? Some specific questions are:

- What is the age distribution of the local population and how is it changing?

- Are any specific groups of people likely to increase or decrease in number?

- Are people leaving the community in greater numbers than they are coming in?

- Where are they coming from and going to?

Knowing where people are moving from and to can help a community or a state prepare for the future. For example, if local retirees are migrating to communities in the Sun Belt, community leaders might try to offer better services for the elderly. If, on the other hand, people of working age are leaving to find jobs in urban areas, the best strategy might be to give more support to businesses that expand job opportunities for the local labor force.

Using its master file of all income tax returns, the Internal Revenue Service counts the number of in- and out-migrants to and from all U.S. counties and states for every two-year period. For each county, the agency calculates how many people moved in (and where they came from) and how many moved out (and where they went). Computer printouts of these data are available for $6.00/county from the IRS, Statistics of Income Division, CP:S, P.O. Box 2608, Washington, DC 20013-2608, (202) 874-0410.

In between the decennial censuses, the first place to look for answers to questions like these is a new series called Population Paper Listings (PPL). This series replaces reports in the P-25 series. It consists of computer-generated printouts and electronic media (diskettes) that data users purchase on a per-request basis.

The PPL series is produced by a cooperative Federal and state program that estimates the population of states, counties, and metropolitan areas annually, and the population of places and other governmental units every two years. Data are available separately for each state, two to three years after the reference period. The estimates are benchmarked on census data (that is, census data are used as reference points) and are developed using administrative records from state health departments, the Internal Revenue Service, and other agencies. For a list of PPL printouts and diskettes, contact the Population Division, Statistical Information staff at (301) 457-2422.

Table 1 uses PPL data to show 1990–1992 population levels for the six sample counties. Note that these numbers are estimates and should be interpreted with care (see box on page 43).

How did it happen that three counties gained and three counties lost population between 1990 and 1992? To answer this question, we look at two components of population change—natural change and net migration.

Natural change is the difference between the number of births and the number of deaths. Fertility, population age structure, and life expectancy all affect the rate of natural change. All other things being equal, a younger population will experience a larger (positive) natural change than an older population.

Table 2 shows the 1990–1992 components of population change for the six sample counties, again using PPL data. All the sample counties, except Yavapai, experienced natural increases in population. They did not all gain population, however, because of *net migration*, the second and most variable

Table 1 The Census Bureau works with individual states to make annual population estimates for all U.S. counties.

County	April 1990 (census)	July 1991 (estimate)	July 1992 (estimate)	Change (estimate)
Attala, MS	18,481	18,515	18,382	-99
Coos, NH	34,828	34,742	34,372	-456
Kossuth, IA	18,591	18,250	18,123	-468
Latah, ID	30,617	31,113	31,768	1,151
Nicholas, WV	26,775	26,748	26,992	217
Yavapai, AZ	107,714	111,871	116,081	8,367

Source: U.S. Department of Commerce, Bureau of the Census (33).

Table 2 Both natural change and net migration contribute to population change.

County	April 1990 (census)	Resident births	Resident deaths	Net natural change	Net migration	Net total change	July 1992 (estimate)
Attala, MS	18,481	672	448	224	-323	-99	18,382
Coos, NH	34,828	946	849	97	-553	-456	34,372
Kossuth, IA	18,591	529	457	72	-540	-468	18,123
Latah, ID	30,617	1,003	432	571	580	1,151	31,768
Nicholas, WV	26,775	738	587	151	66	217	26,992
Yavapai, AZ	107,714	2,723	2,812	-89	8,456	8,367	116,081

Source: U.S. Department of Commerce, Bureau of the Census (37).

An important caveat: Numbers like those in Tables 1 and 2 are only estimates and should be interpreted carefully. In his article, "How to Evaluate Population Estimates," William O'Hare of the Population Reference Bureau provides the following rules of thumb about county and subcounty estimates (11):

- Moderately growing populations can be estimated more accurately than rapidly growing or declining populations.

- Averaging several population estimates (from private data companies, for example) is usually more accurate than relying on only one estimate.

- Adjusting estimates to match an independently derived control total reduces error. This means that population estimates for counties within a state, for example, are more reliable if they are forced to sum to an estimate of the state population that has been derived independently.

- It is easier to estimate changes over a short period of time than over a long period of time.

- The populations of small places are more likely to be overestimated than the populations of larger areas.

---

component of population change. Net migration is the difference between the number of people who move into an area and the number of people who move out. Migration is affected by the economy in the form of employment opportunities—newcomers are attracted by a growing economy that provides more jobs, while people are likely to leave and look for jobs elsewhere when the economy is shrinking.

Attala, Coos, and Kossuth counties experienced net out-migration between 1990 and 1992 (Table 2). In Latah, Nicholas, and Yavapai counties, however, net migration was positive; the number of people moving in was greater than the number moving out.

Natural change and migration work together to determine net total change. In Attala, Coos, and Kossuth counties, natural increase was not large enough to compensate for net out-migration between 1990 and 1992; therefore population decreased. In Yavapai County, in-migration more than compensated for the natural decrease, resulting in a positive net total change of over 8 percent. Latah and Nicholas counties experienced natural increase *and* net in-migration, and therefore their total populations increased 4 percent and 1 percent, respectively.

Because age distribution is so important in explaining both population change and the kinds of goods and services needed by local residents, most states make county-level, age group estimates in between the censuses. A common way of presenting these data is to use an age pyramid like the one in Figure 11. Here, data from the Arizona State Data Center are used to illustrate the age structure of Yavapai County. As a services-dependent, retirement-destination county, Yavapai has relatively few young people, and a relatively high proportion of older residents.

Figure 11   State analysts make intercensal estimates of population age structure.

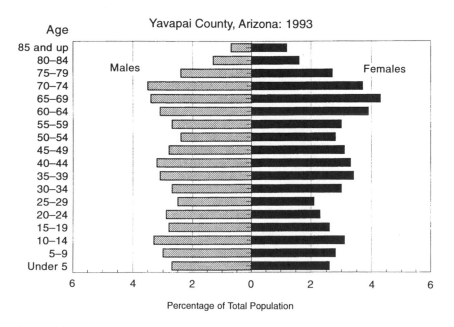

Source: Arizona Department of Economic Security (1).

Education

Education is an investment that brings economic returns both to the individual and to society as a whole. Rural communities are paying particular attention to education in the 1990s as they strive to improve the quality of the local labor force, attract new industries, and diversify their economies.

Commonly asked questions about local education concern attainment, enrollment, finance, and achievement. For example:

- How many adults have completed high school? How many have completed four years of college?

- Is school enrollment changing so that we may need fewer (or more) schools and teachers?

- What percentage of the community's school system revenues come from local sources?

- How well do local test scores compare to those of students in other communities?

Attainment data measure years of school completed. For substate regions, they are available only from the decennial census and are provided for persons in the 18–24 year age range and for those 25 years of age and older. The Census Bureau tabulates attainment data by a variety of demographic characteristics, including sex, race, and rural/urban residence status. Figure 12 illustrates how these data can be used.

As we can see, the populations of Attala and Latah counties differ dramatically in terms of educational attainment. In Attala, the nonspecialized, persistent-poverty county, 21 percent of adults age 25 and over have completed less than nine years of school. Thirteen percent have finished college. In Latah, the government county whose economy largely depends on a land grant university, only five percent have completed less than nine years of school, and 43 percent have completed college.

To get up-to-date enrollment data for a particular community, the best place to go is the local school system. Researchers who want to compare data from different areas can use the *County and City Data Book* (*CCDB*). (Table 3 shows 1990 enrollment

The primary Federal source of education data is the National Center for Education Statistics (NCES). NCES is housed in the Office of Educational Research and Improvement (OERI) in the Department of Education. Information Services, another division of the OERI, handles all requests for data generated by NCES. If you want information about national trends and the latest education research, call (800) 424-1616 to have your name placed on the mailing list for free publications.

Figure 12   The decennial census is the only source of educational attainment data for counties and subcounty areas.

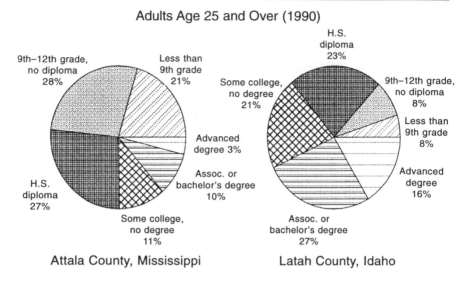

Adults Age 25 and Over (1990)

Attala County, Mississippi

9th–12th grade, no diploma 28%
Less than 9th grade 21%
Advanced degree 3%
Assoc. or bachelor's degree 10%
H.S. diploma 27%
Some college, no degree 11%

Latah County, Idaho

H.S. diploma 23%
Some college, no degree 21%
9th–12th grade, no diploma 8%
Less than 9th grade 8%
Advanced degree 16%
Assoc. or bachelor's degree 27%

Source: U.S. Department of Commerce, Bureau of the Census (<u>42</u>).

Table 3   The Census Bureau publishes school enrollment data in its *County and City Data Book*

| County | Elementary and High School enrollment, 1990 | | High School dropouts[a] |
	Total	Percent Public	
Attala, MS	3,604	91.8	125
Coos, NH	5,875	95.1	163
Kossuth, IA	3,626	78.8	34
Latah, ID	4,640	90.5	55
Nicholas, WV	5,300	97.3	239
Yavapai, AZ	15,243	95.3	617

[a]*CCDB* presents these data on the basis of the county in which the district school superintendent's office is located. Because some districts cross county lines, the county affiliation is not always accurate. High school dropouts are persons 16 to 19 years old not enrolled in school and not high school graduates.

Source: U.S. Department of Commerce, Bureau of the Census (<u>29</u>).

data from the *CCDB* for the six sample counties.) Alternatively, they can contact an agency within the U.S. Department of Education called the National Center for Education Statistics (NCES). NCES collects enrollment data from the states and publishes state totals in their annual report, *Digest of Education Statistics*. District-level data are available from NCES on a paid request basis.

The Office of Educational Research and Improvement (OERI) published a report in 1994 titled "The Condition of Education in Rural Schools." It summarizes research on a variety of issues related to rural schools, including Federal and state policy, conditions for educators, and student performance. Supporting tables include state, regional, and national data on a variety of indicators—for example, the number of rural schools by enrollment size, percentage of public school students enrolled in rural schools, and availability of courses. The report is available for $10 from the Superintendent of Documents, U.S. Government Printing Office (stock number 065-000-00653-7).

Finance is another important education issue. The Census Bureau collects some school finance data in the Census of Governments, which is conducted in years ending in "2" and "7." The *Compendium of Government Finances*, for example, reports total and per capita expenditures on education and libraries (see Chapter 5).

More detailed finance data are typically available from state education agencies. Specifically, these agencies should be able to provide district-level information about how much school funding comes from local, state, and Federal sources, and how much money is spent per pupil on materials, administration, and instruction. (NCES publishes similar data for states.)

Finally, researchers may be interested in data on students' achievement or proficiency in various skills. These data come from standardized tests (the Scholastic Aptitude Test, for example) and are usually collected for individ-

---

NCES conducts a variety of national surveys (both annual and longitudinal) to measure the health of the nation's educational system. Some of its data files allow analyses by metro/nonmetro status. The annual report called *The Condition of Education*, for example, includes selected indicators for schools classified as rural, suburban, and urban. Researchers interested in obtaining data on specific characteristics of schools in rural communities should contact NCES directly. The agency also publishes a variety of reports on school finance and attainment, and some data are available electronically on tape. For a listing, consult the periodic reports, *Programs and Plans of the National Center for Education Statistics* and "Current and Forthcoming Publications." Both reports are available free of charge from NCES while supplies last. Call (800) 424-1616.

ual districts by state education agencies. People who want to compare their district to larger areas should consult the NCES report *Digest of Education Statistics*. The National Assessment of Educational Progress (NAEP) is another NCES program that monitors the skills of primary and secondary students in a variety of subjects (as well as data about school and teacher characteristics). The NAEP survey yields state-level data and is conducted every other year. Reports based on NAEP survey data usually carry the title *The Nation's Report Card* and are available in depository libraries or through NCES.

Labor Force

Economic development in a community is governed partly by the number and characteristics of people who work and the types of jobs they do—whether they are secretaries or doctors, mechanics or librarians. Development is also related to the industries that employ local residents. (Industrial structure is discussed in Chapter 4.) Questions that might be asked about the local labor force include:

- How many people are either working or looking for work?
- Are certain groups of people either coming into or leaving the labor force?
- What is the occupational makeup of the local labor force?

The first place to look for detailed labor force data is the decennial census. The Census Bureau classifies all persons who are at least 16 years old as either in the labor force (that is, in the armed forces, employed in the civilian labor force, unemployed, or actively seeking employment) or out of the labor force. County and some subcounty data are reported by sex, race, type of community (rural/urban), and type of residence (farm/nonfarm). Table 4 illustrates how these data are presented for Nicholas and Kossuth counties.

The labor force participation rate—that is, the percentage of people who are working or looking for work—is one indicator of potential economic growth. A low rate suggests that increased job opportunities could draw more people into the work force, while a higher rate indicates that few additional people may be willing or able to work. In Nicholas County, the la-

> The decennial census is the *only* source of small-area data on employment by occupation. Many states supplement census occupation statistics with state-level estimates. Contact your state employment security agency for more information (see Appendix D).

Table 4 The decennial census provides demographic details about the local labor force.

	1990	
Item	Nicholas County	Kossuth County
Persons 16 years and older	20,328	13,932
Armed Forces	8	7
Civilian labor force	9,934	8,473
Percentage of persons 16 years and older[a]	49	61
Employed	8,575	8,153
Unemployed	1,359	320
Percentage of civilian labor force	14	4
Not in labor force	10,386	5,452
Males 16 to 19 years	858	412
Employed	156	152
Unemployed	91	13
Percentage of males 16 to 19 years old who are in the labor force and unemployed	37	8
Not in labor force	611	247

[a]Labor force participation rate.
Source: U.S. Department of Commerce, Bureau of the Census (42).

bor force participation rate for persons 16 and older is 49 percent. In Kossuth, it is 61 percent.

The decennial census also provides extensive information on characteristics of employment, including detailed occupational groups (types of jobs), detailed industry groups (types of employers), and six classifications of weeks worked per year. These data give researchers their most precise picture of where and how much people are working. Figure 13 shows how we can use occupational data from the decennial census to compare jobs held by rural and urban residents in Latah County. In general, rural people are more likely than urban people to have blue collar occupations, like those classified as "production, craft, and repair" and "operators, fabricators, and laborers."

More up-to-date information about labor force status is available at the county level from the Bureau of Labor Statistics (BLS), which estimates the size of the total labor force and the number of employed and unemployed residents on a monthly and annual basis. These statistics are issued several months after the reference period on microfiche in the series *Unemployment in States and Local Areas*. Table 5 illustrates how these data are presented for Kossuth County.

Figure 13   The decennial census provides detailed information on the types of
jobs people have.

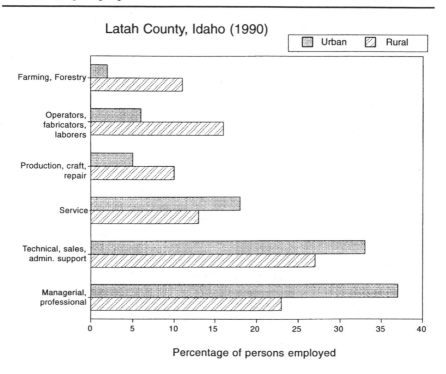

Latah County, Idaho (1990)

Percentage of persons employed

Source: U.S. Department of Commerce, Bureau of the Census (<u>42</u>).

Table 5 BLS works with the states to make labor force estimates for counties.

	Kossuth County, Iowa (January–June, 1992)			
	Persons in labor force	Employed persons	Unemployed persons	Unemployment rate[a]
January	9,124	8,450	674	7.4
February	8,978	8,324	654	7.3
March	9,029	8,333	696	7.7
April	8,828	8,387	441	5.0
May	8,937	8,506	431	4.8
June	9,193	8,773	420	4.6

[a]Percentage of persons in the labor force who are unemployed.
Source: U.S. Department of Labor, Bureau of Labor Statistics (<u>47</u>).

BLS publishes up-to-date labor force data in the quarterly report called *Employment and Earnings* and will include rural data starting in 1996. BLS's annual report, *Geographic Profile of Employment and Unemployment*, contains state-level labor force and demographic data that allow researchers to answer questions about the characteristics of people who are working and of those who are unemployed, and questions about occupations and industries in which the unemployment rate is especially high. BLS's *Monthly Labor Review* (*MLR*) provides recent research results as well as BLS statistical updates. For example, the June 1994 issue included three articles that focused on the effects of the recession; while other articles discussed married mothers' work patterns; growth of jobs in the poultry industry; and current statistics on labor force, productivity, and injury and illness. *MLR* is available from BLS for $25/year. Check the depository library nearest you for these publications.

The Federal government allocates funds for its employment and economic development programs on the basis of BLS unemployment estimates like those in Table 5. BLS works with the states to make these estimates. Estimation procedures are explained in each issue of the periodical *Employment and Earnings*. BLS cautions data users about using its estimates for historical analyses, particularly at the county level or over time periods during which the agency has changed its data collection methods.

In addition to being available on microfiche, recent BLS county-level labor force estimates are also published in the *County and City Data Book* and in reports by state employment security agencies; they are also available through Internet (see Appendix F) or by calling BLS at (202) 606-6391.

Income

Income statistics are widely used measures of economic well-being, but which statistic is most useful depends on the particular research question. For example, it might be important to know:

- How much total income does the community receive and what is the average or per capita income?

- How evenly is this income distributed among local residents?

- Where does local income originate? Do people earn it, receive it from the government, or does it come in the form of property income (like interest)?

To answer questions like these, it is important to understand what each income statistic actually measures.

Personal income, a figure reported by the Bureau of Economic Analysis, is the broadest measure of income. It is defined as the total income, both earned income (such as wages) and unearned income (such as interest), received by, or on behalf of, all residents of a particular area. Hence, BEA's total personal income estimates measure how much money local residents have available to spend before taxes (for example, state and Federal income taxes and individual contributions to Social Security).

Total personal income does not measure how individuals or families are faring, in so far as an increase in total income, for example, could result from an increase in population. Thus we use *per capita* personal income (total personal income divided by population) to indicate the relative level of an area's income, controlled for the population of the area.

The Census Bureau uses a different concept of income, that is, money income. *Money income* is the sum of all cash income, including wages and salaries, net self-employment income, interest, dividends, rent, Social Security payments, public assistance, and other minor types of income. *Earnings income* is reported before personal income taxes, Social Security, etc.

The Census Bureau reports median and mean family income, as well as per capita income. *Median income* is the middle level, that is, the level at which half of the population have lower incomes and half have higher incomes. *Mean income* is the average amount of income received by each family (total money income divided by the number of families).[5]

BEA's personal income is more comprehensive than the Census Bureau's money income for two reasons. First, personal income is based on administrative government records, while money income is based on income reported by individuals (and households or families) in response to surveys or censuses. Money income, therefore, depends on accurate estimates by the respondents. Second, personal income includes some noncash components, such as the value of fringe benefits received by workers but paid by employers, and return on investment in an owner-occupied home. Because of these differences, personal income estimates for an area are usually higher than money income estimates.

Another widely used income measure is the percentage of the population (individuals, households, or families) that have money income below the poverty level—the so-called *poverty rate*. Each year, the U.S. Office of Management and Budget (OMB) establishes a series of poverty income thresholds for different family sizes, ages of household heads, and geo-

---

[5]Household income is sometimes used instead of family income. A household consists of all people living in a single dwelling, whereas a family consists of two or more related individuals.

graphic locations. These poverty thresholds come from an index developed in 1964 by the Social Security Administration. The index is based on evidence from the USDA's 1955 Survey of Food Consumption that found families with three or more people spend roughly one-third of their money income on food. Hence, the poverty level for these families was set at three times the cost of the so-called "economy food plan," with modifications for smaller families. Many analysts consider this method of measuring poverty to be outdated (in part because of the assumption about how much money is spent on food), but they have not been able to agree on a more satisfactory method.

Each year, OMB revises its poverty thresholds to reflect changes in the Consumer Price Index (CPI). This means that poverty rates can be compared from one time period to the next. When using other income measures, it is always important to find out whether they are expressed in *real* (sometimes called *constant*) dollars, which are adjusted by an index such as the CPI, or in *current*, unadjusted dollars. In addition, researchers should note that income measures are rarely adjusted by an index that reflects price changes in individual regions or subpopulations. The CPI, for example, is derived at the national level.[6]

In summary, there are several commonly used income statistics, total and per capita personal income, mean and median money income, and the poverty rate. In the following section, we illustrate how these statistics can be used.

Bureau of the Census

Based on sample data collected in the decennial census, the Census Bureau estimates four money income measures at the county level: mean income, median income, per capita income, and percentage below poverty. Data are provided for persons and families and, in some cases, for households. At the county level, these statistics are only available every ten years and are not available from any other public source.

As noted above, the Census Bureau estimates of money income are based on people's responses to the decennial census long form questionnaire. Money income excludes nonmonetary income, such as the value of food stamps, housing subsidies, and employers' pension contributions. It also excludes one-time income such as loans and capital gains or losses.

Table 6 illustrates how we can use Census data to find out the number and

---

[6]BLS actually derives an index of price change for two population groups—one for urban consumers (CPI-U) and one for urban wage earners and clerical workers (CPI-W). The CPI-U is used to adjust income figures. No specific accounting of price change for rural consumers is made. For more information, see (46).

Table 6 The decennial census provides small-area data on the number and characteristics of poor people.

Item	Attala County, Mississippi (1989)				
	Total	White	Black	Rural	Farm
Total number of persons	18,481	11,081	7,329	11,501	376
Persons with income					
below poverty	5,512	1,955	3,525	3,532	84
Poverty rate	30%	18%	48%	31%	22%
Total number of families	5,058	3,247	1,801	3,211	117
Families with income					
below poverty	1,272	431	841	820	14
Poverty rate	25%	13%	47%	26%	12%

Source: U.S. Department of Commerce, Bureau of the Census (Tables 6, 149, 158, 215, 217, 219, 221) (42).

Consumer Income **(Series P-60 from the Census Bureau) is the best source of intercensal income estimates for individuals, families, and households in the United States.** Based on the March supplement to the Current Population Survey, *Consumer Income* enables us to follow trends in the level and distribution of income, and in the characteristics of people at different income levels. All estimates are presented for the nation as a whole, and selected estimates appear for regions, states, and by metro/nonmetro residence.

Researchers interested in poverty, for example, can refer to the P-60 report, *Income, Poverty, and Valuation of Noncash Benefits.* (This report combines three previous publications: *Money Income and Poverty Status of Persons in the United States, Valuation of Noncash Benefits,* and *Poverty in the United States.)* Some of the questions that can be answered using this report are:

- How does the poverty rate in nonmetro counties compare to that for inner cities?

- What are the demographic characteristics of people who are most likely to be poor? For example, in which region (South or non-South) do they live, how large are their families, and how old are they?

P-60 reports are issued periodically. Because of funding cuts, fewer data tables will be published in the combined report than in the previous three. More detailed data can be ordered by phone on a cost-per-request basis from the Poverty and Wealth Branch at (301) 763-8578, or from the Income Branch of the Housing and Household Economic Statistics Division at the Census Bureau at (301) 763-8576. Portions of the reports are also available electronically via Internet (see Appendix F). Contact Customer Services at (301) 457-4100 to order individual reports.

Between decennial census years we often want to know the poverty rate for areas smaller than those covered by Census Bureau publications. Researchers use several techniques for estimating these statistics. Some start with decennial census data on the social and economic characteristics associated with being poor. Then they make more current county estimates based on the presence of these particular characteristics in the local population. Others use data from the Current Population Survey to make estimates, either for one specific year at the state level or for a several-year average for specific demographic groups in individual states. (See (9), (12), and (14) for examples of these techniques.)

All of these analyses should be regarded with great caution. They are estimates based on estimates, since decennial census poverty statistics are derived from a sample rather than the whole population. Hence, they are subject to multiple sources of error. Nevertheless, they are useful as approximations and may be very helpful in guiding program and policy development in the absence of more precise statistics.

characteristics of people with income below the poverty level. In 1989, 30 percent of all persons in Attala County had income less than the poverty level, compared to 13 percent nationwide. Poor people in Attala County were disproportionately black, and farm residents were less likely to be poor than other rural residents. Note that the data refer to 1989, the year before the most recent decennial census. This is because respondents answered the question, "What was your total income from all sources in the last year?"

Between past decennial censuses, the Census Bureau has published its irregular P-25 series, *Local Population Estimates*. P-25 reports included population and per capita income estimates for counties and subcounty areas. Unfortunately, the series has been temporarily discontinued while the Census Bureau revises its estimation methodology. Call the Housing and Household Economic Characteristics Division (Small Area Income and Poverty Statistics staff) at (301) 763-8413 for more information on what is currently available.

The Census Bureau reports its larger area, intercensal income estimates in *Consumer Income*, Series P-60. These reports are based on the March supplement to the Current Population Survey. They provide information about people at various income levels and on the relationship of income to age, sex, race, family size, education, occupation, and other characteristics.

Bureau of Economic Analysis

The Bureau of Economic Analysis also reports income data that are useful for analyzing nonmetro counties. These county-level data are by-products of BEA's responsibility to monitor and measure the performance of the national

BEA distributes a CD-ROM called *Regional Economic Information System.* Updated each year, the CD-ROM contains data on total and per capita personal income, income by type, and earnings by type and major industry. Data are presented for the United States, eight BEA regions, states, and counties. Earnings data are reported at the 2-digit SIC level for states and the 1-digit level for counties. (See Chapter 2 for information about the SIC coding system.) Also available on CD-ROM for counties are component estimates of transfer payments, farm income and expenditures, and full- and part-time employment by 1-digit SIC. The CD-ROM is available from BEA user groups in each state and from Federal depository libraries; its cost is $35. To order, call REIS at (202) 606-5360, or write to the Public Information Office, Order Desk, BE-53, Bureau of Economic Analysis, 1441 L St. NW, U.S. Department of Commerce, Washington, DC 20230.

economy.[7] The agency's county estimates are widely used to evaluate the impact of public programs, allocate Federal funds, project tax revenues, and evaluate markets for new products. Researchers can use the estimates to measure and track income received by the local population and as a framework for analyzing the local economy.

Each year and for all counties, BEA tabulates total personal income, which is current income received by residents from all sources. The agency measures personal income before taxes (like the Census Bureau) but after contributions to various retirement programs. Unlike the Census Bureau, BEA includes some noncash income such as food stamps and employer-paid health insurance. The agency reports personal income by source on a *place-of-residence* basis. This means, for example, that income data are reported for people who live in Coos County, not for people who work in Coos County. The two groups of people are different if workers commute across county lines.

The major categories of income included in the BEA data are:

• Earnings (wage and salary income, proprietors' income from farm
   and nonfarm sources, and various employer contributions);

---

[7]BEA issues its national estimates of personal income first, on a monthly basis, within a few weeks of the end of every month. State-level personal income estimates are issued on a quarterly basis, approximately two months after the end of the previous quarter—at which time the national estimates are already being revised. State-level annual personal income estimates are issued about six months after the end of the calendar year, with estimates for several previous years revised at the same time. Finally, county-level estimates are released about 18 months after the year to which they refer, at which time the estimates for several previous years are also revised. If you need recent quarterly estimates that have not been released on CD-ROM, contact BEA's Regional Economic Information System (REIS) or a BEA user group.

- Personal investment income (dividends, interest, and rent); and
- Transfer payments (retirement-related, unemployment insurance, public assistance, and miscellaneous).

BEA obtains most of its wage and salary data from tax and statistical records supplied by state employment security agencies. Aggregate data on nonfarm proprietors' income are obtained primarily from the Internal Revenue Service. (The IRS does not release individual tax returns.) Farm proprietors' income estimates are based on IRS aggregates, Census of Agriculture county data, and selected annual county data prepared by the state offices affiliated with USDA's National Agricultural Statistics Service (NASS).

BEA estimates data on transfer payments, investment income, and proprietors' income on a place-of-residence basis. It estimates data on other components of earnings (wages and salaries, other labor income, and employer contributions) on a place-of-work basis. To reconcile these differences, the agency makes adjustments that reflect the intercounty commuting patterns reported in each decennial census.

Figure 14 BEA estimates per capita personal income by source.

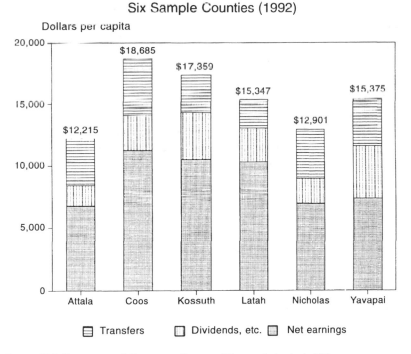

Six Sample Counties (1992)

Dollars per capita

☐ Transfers   ☐ Dividends, etc.   ☐ Net earnings

Source: U.S. Department of Commerce, Bureau of Economic Analysis (45).

Figure 15   BEA provides detailed component estimates of government transfer
payments.

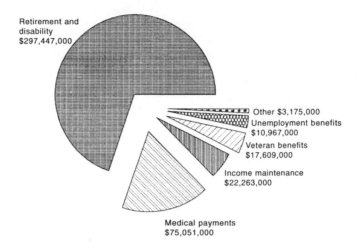

Yavapai County, Arizona (1992)

Retirement and
disability
$297,447,000

Other $3,175,000
Unemployment benefits
$10,967,000
Veteran benefits
$17,609,000
Income maintenance
$22,263,000

Medical payments
$75,051,000

Source: U.S. Department of Commerce, Bureau of Economic Analysis (45).

The advantage of BEA data is that they are comprehensive, reported in
great detail, and readily accessible through BEA user groups. The disadvantage is that they are based on administrative and survey data collected by
other agencies, and as such they reflect an assortment of complex adjustments. Call REIS staff at (202) 606-5360 if you need information about how
various adjustments are made.

Figure 14 shows how researchers can use BEA personal income data to
better understand the relative importance of various income sources.

BEA also makes detailed county-level estimates of various types of transfer payments. Community leaders and development practitioners are becoming more aware of the economic stimulus provided by such payments,
including retirement income and welfare benefits. Figure 15 shows, for
example, that retirement and disability insurance is the largest component of
transfer payments in Yavapai County, accounting for over two-thirds of total
government transfers. Income maintenance payments (such as public assistance) are a small component, accounting for only about five percent.

Social Security Administration

Each year, the Social Security Administration (SSA) publishes information about beneficiaries of the Old Age, Survivors, and Disability Insurance

Program (OASDI). The data include the number of beneficiaries in each state, county, and zip code, and the aggregate dollar amount of benefits by type. (See the reports *OASDI Beneficiaries by State and County* and *OASDI Beneficiaries by ZIP Code.*) Using administrative data, SSA reports these numbers roughly 12 months after the reference year. Researchers can use the information if they want more detail on retirement and disability income than BEA provides. (BEA reports the same data in *REIS*, but in less detail.) Not all of the SSA publications use the same methods to avoid disclosing data, so read the introduction to each report before using the data or contact SSA staff listed in the front of each report. For ordering information, write to the Chief of Publications Staff, Office of Research and Statistics, Social Security Administration, 4301 Connecticut Ave. NW, Room 209, Washington, DC 20008.

Housing

Some research indicates that substandard housing is more common in rural areas than in urban areas, but measuring the quantity and quality of housing in small communities is complicated by a lack of data. The Census Bureau, for example, only reports information on housing units that are occupied year-round, and thus neglects units that are seasonally occupied by migrant workers. Further, the Census Bureau limits its questions on housing quality to inquiries about the presence of selected facilities and equipment. Broader indicators of housing quality—such as structural deficiency—are available only from the American Housing Survey (AHS). Unfortunately, the AHS sample is too small to provide geographical detail for particular rural communities.

Evaluating the quality of rural housing is also limited by our ability to objectively measure what constitutes "substandard" housing. The Housing Assistance Council (HAC) notes, for example, that while the number of rural

---

The American Housing Survey is a good source of larger-area rural housing data. The AHS is conducted jointly by the Office of Policy Development and Research of the U.S. Department of Housing and Urban Development and the Bureau of the Census. The AHS provides urban/rural and metro/nonmetro cross tabulations by geographic region. Every four years, extra cases are added to the sample in rural areas to produce better estimates of rural housing characteristics. The AHS is particularly useful in that it provides more data on housing quality than the decennial census. AHS reports are published biennially on a regional basis in the Census Bureau Series H-150.

Housing Characteristics of Rural Households: 1991 (H-121-93-5) is
one of the Current Housing Reports issued jointly by the Census Bureau
and the U.S. Department of Housing and Urban Development. It contains
data for the United States and regions on the geographic distribution and
physical characteristics of rural housing, as well as on the social and economic characteristics of rural householders. Data are presented for rural
places that are: inside and outside metro areas; adjacent and nonadjacent to metro areas; and farm and nonfarm. The report costs $4 and can
be ordered from Customer Services at (301) 457-4100.

housing units without plumbing facilities and the number that are over-
crowded has clearly declined in recent years, the number of mobile homes
has increased dramatically. HAC suggests that mobile homes may not be
substandard in the traditional sense, but the national standards that regulate
their construction do not uniformly guarantee durability or thermal protection. Hence mobile homes are often of lower "quality" than conventional
housing (7).

With these shortcomings in mind, researchers can begin to describe the
quantity and quality of rural housing. In trying to design effective housing
development strategies, community leaders might ask questions like the following:

• Do the size and characteristics of local housing units meet the needs
  of residents?

• Do residents own or rent their homes?

• What is the quality of the local housing and how has it changed in
  recent years?

In general, the data we use to answer these questions are available from the
decennial census. Between censuses, local planning and community action
agencies can often provide more up-to-date information. For more details,
see United States Department of Commerce, Bureau of the Census, "American Housing Survey: Housing Data Between the Censuses," 1992 (22).

The first place to look for information about the number and characteristics of local housing units is the decennial census. According to the Census
Bureau, a *housing unit* is "a house, apartment, flat, mobile home, a group of
rooms, or a single room, occupied or intended for occupancy as separate living quarters; that is, the occupants do not live and eat with any other persons
in the building, and there is direct access to the unit from the outside or from
a common hall" (22). The Census Bureau tabulated a complete count of all
housing units from its 1990 census, available down to the block level. All

respondents were asked whether they live in a mobile home or trailer, one-family house, or apartment building.

Researchers can make more current estimates of housing numbers by updating census data with other sources of information. Information on the number of building permits issued is published in the *CCDB* and is usually available from state and local sources. For example, the New Hampshire Office of State Planning (OSP) regularly updates Census figures using resi-dential building permits and annually publishes estimates of the housing numbers in each township (10). Figure 16 shows the OSP data for Coos County.

The agency estimates that the number of housing units in all three cate-gories—single family, multi-family, and mobile homes—increased between 1990 and 1992. On the other hand, the Census Bureau estimates the number of people in Coos County decreased during this period (Table 1). More

Figure 16   Some states estimate housing numbers by using building permit data.

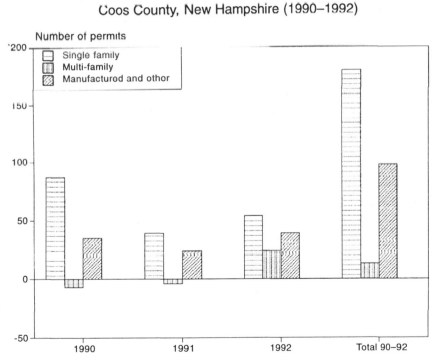

Coos County, New Hampshire (1990–1992)

(negative numbers represent conversions)

Source: New Hampshire Office of State Planning (10).

research might help us decide whether these divergent trends were due to fewer people living in each housing unit, the construction of vacation homes, or some other factor.

After learning about the size and characteristics of local housing units, the next thing researchers may want to measure is the quality of housing in a particular community. The size of housing units relative to the number of occupants is one commonly used measure of quality. Small-area data on overcrowding (defined as more than one person per room) are available from the decennial census on a complete count basis.

The presence and condition of particular facilities and equipment are also frequently used indicators of housing quality. Because lack of plumbing facilities is usually associated with substandard housing, the most widely used and objective measure of quality is the presence of complete plumbing facilities for exclusive use of the household. (Complete plumbing facilities include hot and cold piped water, a flush toilet, and a bathtub or shower.) Other facilities and equipment that may indicate housing quality are complete kitchen facilities, telephone, central heat, and public water hookup. Care should be used in interpreting these indicators; however, as none by itself is a complete measure of housing quality. Relevant data are available from the decennial census for small areas (on a sample basis from the 1990 census) and from the American Housing Survey for regions.

Health

Rural communities face two major health issues: (1) the health status of the population and (2) access to health resources, that is, to health care providers, facilities, and services. Public concern about these two issues has increased in recent years because of research documenting the effects of poverty and environmental pollution on health, and because many rural health care providers face growing financial problems. Very few small-area statistics on

---

Information for Action: An Advocate's Guide to Using Maternal and Child Health Data, published by the Children's Defense Fund, is an excellent resource for community researchers. This very readable book includes topics on ways to approach health-related research questions, choosing indicators, accessing state and local data sources, and presenting research results. It costs $6.95. To order this publication, contact the Children's Defense Fund, 25 E Street, NW, Washington, DC 20001, or call (202) 628-8787.

The **Rural Information Center Health Service (RICHS)** is a part of the Rural Information Center (RIC) at the National Agricultural Library (NAL). RICHS was created in 1990 by the NAL and the Office of Rural Health Policy in the Department of Health and Human Services to provide information on rural health. Services include literature searches on rural health issues, help in locating information, and referrals to organizations or individuals who can assist with specialized information. RICHS has a conference on the NAL's Agricultural Library Forum (ALF) bulletin board that includes information on rural health publications, national and state conferences, and agricultural safety and health programs. (See Appendix F for information on accessing ALF.) Contact RICHS staff at the Rural Information Center, National Agricultural Library, Room 304, 10301 Baltimore Blvd., Beltsville, MD 20705-2351; or call (800) 633-7701, or (301) 504-5547 in the Washington, DC area; or e-mail through Internet (see Appendix F).

health status are published at the Federal level so the best place to start looking for information on health status is the local or state public health agency.

Information about access to health resources is somewhat easier to obtain. *AHA Hospital Statistics* reports data compiled from the American Hospital Association's Annual Survey of Hospitals. It provides information for Census divisions and states on the number of hospitals and nursing homes, their size (number of beds), and type of facility (for example, psychiatric or chronic disease). It also includes financial information such as the type of ownership (private, nonprofit, government), number of full-time employees, and payroll. Another report, *AHA Guide to the Health Care Field,* provides more detailed data, but for each hospital that responded to the AHA's Annual Survey of Hospitals. The data are organized by state and city, and each entry lists the county where the hospital is located. Each report includes contacts who can answer specific questions about methodology or content.

Physician Characteristics and Distribution in the U.S. is an annual report published by the American Medical Association. It includes state and county group data on the number of physicians, individual characteristics (including age and gender), and area of specialization (for example, family practice or pediatrics). The report includes a table which identifies counties without an active physician. Check your nearest depository library or health-related library for these publications.

Health United States is an annual report published by the National Center for Health Statistics that provides national-level data on a variety of health-related subjects, including health care resources and expenditures. Some state-level data are provided, such as the number of hospital beds per capita and per capita expenditures for mental health services.

Limited county-level data on health status and resources are published in the *County and City Data Book,* as illustrated in Table 7.

Table 7 The *County and City Data Book* includes limited health status and resource data.

Item	Attala County, Mississippi	Kossuth County, Iowa
Population by race (1990)		
White (%)	60.1	99.3
Black (%)	39.5	0.0
Other (%)	0.3	0.4
Number of hospital beds (1991)	76	29
Active, non-Federal physicians		
Number, 1990	15	6
Number per 100,000 residents as of April 1, 1990	81	32
Infant mortality rate[a]	10.9	8.2

[a]Deaths of infants under one-year old per 1,000 live births.
Source: U.S. Department of Commerce, Bureau of the Census (29).

4

Understanding the Economies of Rural Communities

Overview of Local Economic Structure

Our sample counties reflect the diverse economic makeup of rural America, as illustrated in Figure 17. To evaluate alternative development strategies, citizens and policy makers need to understand their local economic structure, in terms of both the contribution that various industries make, and cyclical and structural changes that affect these industries. Critical questions might include:

- How diversified is our economy?

- What industries are most important to residents' economic well-being?

- Do these industries produce goods (like agriculture, mining, and manufacturing) or services (like tourism, trade, and education)?

- Which industries are growing in importance, which are declining, and how do these trends compare to the regional and national economy?

To answer these questions we shift our focus away from data about people and toward data about the industries that make up a community's economy. These industries can be analyzed from the standpoint of both jobs and income, as explained in the rest of this chapter.

Employment
Employment data tell us how many jobs each industry provides for the local economy. The main sources of employment data are:

Figure 17 Researchers can use BEA earnings data to analyze the economic structure of individual counties.

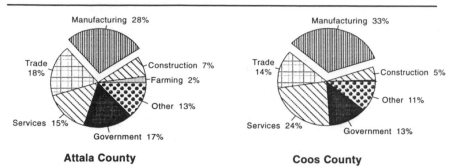

Attala County

Coos County

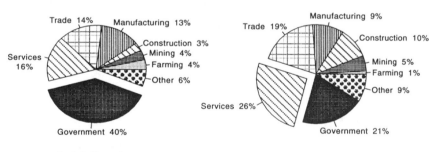

Kossuth County

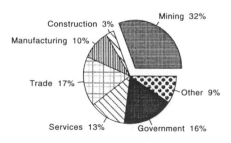

Latah County

Yavapai County

Nicholas County

Source: U.S. Department of Commerce, Bureau of Economic Analysis (45).

- Bureau of the Census (decennial census reports and *County Business Patterns*);
- Bureau of Labor Statistics and State employment security agencies (SESAs); and
- Bureau of Economic Analysis.

We report employment data for Nicholas County in Table 8 and summarize the characteristics of each data source in Table 9. Table 8 shows that the four sources report very different numbers and are not comparable because coverage and definitions vary widely.

Table 8 Four sources of employment statistics for Nicholas County, West Virginia.

	Number of employed persons or jobs[a]			
Industry	1990 Census	1992 County Business Patterns	1993 Employment Security Agency	1992 BEA
Agriculture, forestry, and fisheries	104	NA	27	360
Agricultural services, forestry, and fisheries	NA	30	NA	76
Mining	1,412	1,394	989	1,270
Construction	503	200	245	360
Manufacturing	1,143	808	835	947
Transportation, communication, and public utilities	584	320	391	504
Wholesale trade	196	243	268	384
Retail trade	1,610	1,695	1,724	2,052
Finance, insurance, and real estate	320	239	212	305
Services	2,393	1,048	1,022	1,775
Government	310	NA	1,617	1,800
TOTAL	8,575	5,977	7,330	9,833

[a]Numbers are not directly comparable because coverage and definitions vary by source. See text and Table 9 for details.

Sources: U.S. Department of Commerce, Bureau of the Census (42) and (30); U.S. Department of Commerce, Bureau of Economic Analysis (45); West Virginia Bureau of Employment Programs (49).

Table 9 Which data source is most appropriate depends on the research question.

Data source	Basis	Unit of observation	Where the data originate
Decennial census (Bureau of the Census)	Place of residence (people)	Census respondent	Sample of the population
County Business Patterns (Bureau of the Census)	Place of work (people)	Establishment (single physical location where business is conducted or industrial operations are performed)	Economic censuses, annual economic surveys, and administrative records
Bureau of Labor Statistics and SESAs[b]	Place of work (jobs)	Establishment (economic unit which produces goods or services, generally at a single location)	Quarterly reports filed by employers subject to unemployment insurance laws
Bureau of Economic Analysis	Place of work (jobs)	Same as BLS	Quarterly ES-202 reports and administrative records from other agencies and organizations

[a]When not suppressed. See Chapter 2 for discussion of SIC codes.
[b]SESA: State Employment Security Agencies.
Sources: U.S. Department of Commerce, Bureau of the Census (42) and (30); U.S. Department of Labor, Bureau of Labor Statistics (46); authors' personal communication with staff from Bureau of Economic Analysis, and Bureau of Labor Statistics.

Coverage	Industry detail[a]	Geographic detail	Format	Frequency
All employees and self-employed	4-digit SIC	To county subdivisions	Published, fiche, CD-ROM	Every 10 years; 2–3 years after reference period
Includes employment covered by FICA (primarily private, nonfarm wage and salary). Excludes self-employed persons, government employees, farm workers, and domestic service workers. Government-owned hospitals and liquor stores included.	4-digit SIC	To counties	Published, CD-ROM	Annual; 2–3 years after reference period
Includes workers covered by state unemployment compensation laws and by the Unemployment Compensation for Federal Employees (UCFE) program. Excludes self-employed persons.	4-digit SIC	To counties	Upon request from BLS; upon request and also sometimes published by state employment security agencies	Annual; within 1 year of reference period
Includes private and public, full-time and part-time, self employment and wage and salary employment.	1-digit SIC for full- and part-time employment	To counties	CD-ROM and user groups in each state	Annual; within 18 months of reference period

---

Where to get employment and earnings data for counties

- Look in the library for Census Bureau reports.
- Call your state employment security agency or BLS in Washington, D.C.
- Contact a BEA user group in your state.

  See Appendix D for names and phone numbers.

Find out what's happening in your state—BLS news releases titled "State and Metropolitan Area Employment and Unemployment" and "The Employment Situation" report up-to-date information on employment at the state and national level. Write to the Branch of Inquiries and Correspondence, BLS, Washington, DC 20212-0001 to get on the mailing list.

The decennial census provides the most detailed employment-by-industry data. These data, which are published in *Social and Economic Characteristics* (Series CP-2), are available for counties and county subdivisions and for many industrial classifications. Employment data are cross-tabulated by demographic characteristics, and therefore give researchers the most details about the types of people who work in different industries.

The second column in Table 8 shows summarized 1990 employment data from Series CP-2 for Nicholas County. These data are reported on a place-of-residence basis. This means, for example, that 1,412 people who lived in Nicholas County in 1990 worked in the mining industry, according to the 1990 census. The data represent numbers of people rather than numbers of jobs.

Because the census is taken only every ten years, it does not allow us to track recent changes in economic structure. However, the Census Bureau's annual *County Business Patterns* (*CBP*) provides more recent (but less detailed) employment-by-industry data for counties. The data are obtained from economic censuses, various annual surveys, and administrative records from other agencies. *CBP* reports are issued for each state and include all employment covered by the Federal Insurance Contributions Act (FICA). They do not include data for state or local government employees, self-employed persons, farm workers, or domestic service workers. Hospitals and state-owned liquor establishments, however, are included. Because farmers and their employees are not included, *CBP* is less useful for counties where agriculture is important. (Selected *CBP* data are reported in the *County and City Data Book*.)

For every county, *CBP* tells us how many people work in each industry, what their total payroll is, how many individual establishments make up the industry, and how large these establishments are in terms of employment. Data that would disclose the payroll or precise number of employees for individual employers are not published. (The number of establishments and their distribution by employment-size class are not considered disclosures.) *CBP* does not show separate data for any industry that has fewer than 50 employees, but these data are available by paid request if there is no disclosure problem.

The third column in Table 8 shows *CBP* employment data for Nicholas County. The data are reported according to place-of-work and represent numbers of workers. This means, for example, that 1,394 people who worked in Nicholas County in 1992 were employed in the mining industry, according to *CBP*.

In order to administer the state unemployment insurance programs, the Bureau of Labor Statistics also tabulates employment-by-industry data. These data pertain to virtually all private and government workers.[8] The data come from quarterly tax bills and statistical requests sent by the SESAs to private businesses and government agencies.

BLS does not publish the county data but does make them available by paid request. County statistics are also available from the SESAs, although these agencies vary considerably in how accessible they make the data. One SESA requires data users to come to the state capital and hand-copy data, while others mail computer printouts or published data free of charge. The West Virginia Department of Employment Security, for example, publishes county employment figures annually and mails them free of charge.

The fourth column in Table 8 shows SESA data for Nicholas County. They are reported according to place-of-work and represent numbers of jobs covered by unemployment insurance. This means, for example, that there were 989 jobs in the mining industry in 1993, according to the West Virginia SESA.

The fourth source of employment data is the Bureau of Economic Analysis. The data are available on the *Regional Economic Information System* CD-ROM and from BEA user groups in each state. (Call BEA or your state data center for the user group nearest you.)

The advantage of the BEA series is its broad coverage. Public and private, farm and nonfarm, wage/salary and self-employment are all included. One disadvantage is that some of the information is extrapolated from survey data

---

[8]BLS estimates that this program covers about 99.6 percent of all nonfarm wage and salary workers in the United States and 92 percent of all workers in the economy. The missing 8 percent are almost entirely self-employed. To the extent that rural people are more likely to be self-employed than urban people, the coverage in rural areas is lower.

when administrative data are not available, and so it may be somewhat less reliable. Another disadvantage is that the county data are only available for broad industry groups, that is, at the 1-digit SIC level.

The fifth column in Table 8 illustrates BEA employment-by-industry data for Nicholas County. The data represent numbers of jobs and are reported according to place-of-work. This means, for example, that there were 1,270 jobs in the mining industry in 1992, according to BEA.

Earnings

Earnings data reflect total compensation including wages, salaries, bonuses, and severance pay. Researchers can get up-to-date, county-level wage data from BLS (through the SESAs) and county-level personal income data from BEA.

BLS and its cooperating SESAs collect wage (or payroll) data directly from employers when they gather their employment information, thus the coverage of both public and private sector wage and salary workers is almost complete. Again, BLS only makes these data available at the county level by paid request, and SESAs vary in how accessible they make the data. As with other data, neither the BLS nor SESAs will release any information that would allow an individual employer to be identified.

Table 10 shows data from the West Virginia Bureau of Employment Programs for Nicholas County. Note that the data pertain only to earnings by workers covered by unemployment insurance and therefore do not include proprietors' self-employment income. West Virginia issues the data about eight or nine months after the reference year.

The main reason that SESAs collect covered employment and wage data is to administer unemployment insurance programs. However, analysts at all levels of government and the private sector use the data. The Federal government, for example, uses them to calculate a geographical index for various public assistance programs; state agencies use them to monitor industry trends; and business and labor organizations use them to negotiate wage agreements.

BEA uses BLS earnings data as the earnings component of its comprehensive personal income series. As noted in Chapter 3 and illustrated in Figure 17, BEA personal income data are widely used as a framework for analyzing the structure of local economies. The data are estimated on a place-of-work basis, by type and by industry, in the annual *BEA Regional Economic Information System (REIS)* CD-ROM. Farm earnings are reported separately from nonfarm earnings, and earnings from the private sector are reported separately from public sector earnings. The data are available in published and computerized form; revised estimates are available upon request from BEA.

Table 10 State Employment Security Agencies publish annual data on earnings by industry.

Industry[a]	Number of establishments	Total wages	Average annual wage	Average weekly wage
	Nicholas County, West Virginia (1993)			
Mining	48	$39,376,499	$39,814	$766
Coal mining	47	39,278,973	39,877	767
Manufacturing	41	15,614,301	18,699	360
Lumber and wood products	25	7,468,211	19,862	382
Printing and publishing	3	275,558	9,502	183
Industrial machinery	6	2,086,886	24,843	478
Services	162	15,488,314	15,154	291
Hotels and other lodging places	11	1,212,914	12,251	236
Business services	13	1,388,175	16,725	322
Health services	29	5,872,213	16,176	311
Automotive repairs and services	15	498,750	12,468	240
Miscellaneous repair services	11	693,974	18,756	361
Legal services	12	798,927	15,665	301
Social services	4	1,131,636	11,430	220
Membership organizations	11	124,551	3,277	63
Engineering and management services	25	3,124,308	22,477	432

[a]Only selected industries shown here.
Source: West Virginia Bureau of Employment Programs (49).

Industry-Specific Data

Once researchers have an overview of local economic structure, they may want more information about the individual industries that are important to a community's well-being.[9] Questions that might be asked include:

- What is the structure of our most important industries? Do many relatively small firms compete with each other, or do only a few large firms dominate these industries?
- What is the value of production from these industries?

---

[9]For background on the performance and structure of industries that are important to rural communities, see (17).

- Are these industries becoming more productive; that is, are they producing the same or more output with fewer inputs?

To answer questions like these, researchers can use a combination of data sources, beginning with the employment and earnings sources listed above and with the agricultural and economic censuses conducted in years ending in "2" and "7." These censuses provide data on agriculture, mining, manufacturing, trade, and services for counties and, in some cases, for places with 2,500 or more inhabitants. The agricultural and economic censuses are mandated by law. Firms are required to respond, but are protected by the confidentiality requirement that prevents publication of data that would reveal specific identities and activities. Data are collected on an establishment basis. Firms operating more than one establishment are required to file a separate report for each location. Researchers can supplement small-area data from these sources with information from state- and national-level industry reports, and with data from other government agencies.

What is the national outlook for industries that are important to your community? For information about nonfarm industries, see *U.S. Industrial Outlook,* an annual report from the Department of Commerce. It can be ordered from the Government Printing Office for $37 (stock number 003-009-00635-0) or found in depository libraries. For information about agriculture, see the monthly report from ERS-NASS, *Agricultural Outlook.* A one-year subscription costs $42. Both publications provide detailed information about specific industries. Authors of individual articles are excellent contacts for more information.

The Economic Census' Survey of *Minority-Owned Business Enterprises* and *Survey of Women-Owned Businesses* provide data for counties that have at least 100 businesses owned by women, blacks, Hispanics, or Asian Americans, American Indians, and other minorities. The reports are most useful for counties with a significant population of an ethnic or racial group—for example, Hispanic business owners in Yavapai County, Arizona. Data items include total number of firms (as opposed to establishments, see Glossary), firms with paid employees, sales or receipts, number of employees, and annual payroll. The reports are published in series numbers as follows: women WB-1; black MB-1; Hispanic MB-2; Asian Americans, American Indians, and other minorities MB-3. Reports from the 1992 *Survey* will be released in spring 1995. After published reports are released, data will also be available on CEN-DATA. Check your depository library, or call Customer Services at the Census Bureau for ordering information.

Agriculture

Although many rural communities have diversified their industrial mix in the last several decades, a significant percentage continue to rely heavily on agriculture as a major source of income. Farming-dependent counties, of which there are 556, are concentrated in the Great Plains, with others clustered in the Mississippi Delta and parts of the West. The issues facing people in these communities include farm profitability, the environmental consequences of current farming practices, and the structure of the industry itself. Questions that people might ask include:

- What are the major crops produced and types of livestock raised?
- What is the financial condition of local farmers?
- How big is the average farm?
- How many farms are sole proprietorships (that is, owned by one person), how many are partnerships, and how many are corporations?
- How many farmers are part-time?

Probably because of its historical importance, we have more information about agriculture than about any other industry that contributes to the rural economy. The most comprehensive source is the agricultural census, conducted every five years by the Bureau of the Census but every four years between 1969 and 1982. It is the only source of consistent, comparable agriculture data at the county, state, and national levels.

Published reports from the agricultural census include data on number and size of farms; crop production; livestock, poultry, and their products; tenure, age, and principal occupation of operator; type of organization; value of products sold; production expenses; and many other characteristics.

Results of the 1992 Census of Agriculture are published in Volume 1, Geographic Area Series (AC92-A-1 through AC92-A-51). The reports provide data at the national, state, and county (or equivalent) levels. Results are also available on computer tape, CD-ROM, and online on CENDATA and Internet (see Appendix F). For more information, write the Bureau of the Census, Agriculture and Financial Statistics Division, Washington, DC 20233-8300 or call (800) 523-3215. For additional information about electronic data products, call Customer Services at (301) 457-4100.

For the last census, which was done in 1992, the Census Bureau mailed short "screening" questionnaires to a list of four million individuals, businesses, and organizations that the agency had identified as being associated with agriculture. Respondents were asked questions to determine whether they met USDA's definition of a farm, that is, whether they sold (or had the potential to sell) at least $1,000 worth of agricultural products in 1991. Those that qualified received a complete census questionnaire.

County-level agricultural census data are available in state-by-state reports about two or three years after the reference period. State reports from the 1992 Census were released in 1994.

More up-to-date information about agriculture is available from the National Agricultural Statistics Service (NASS) in USDA. Each year, NASS's 45 field offices conduct sample surveys by mail, telephone, personal interviews, and in-the-field observation to collect information on crop and livestock production, chemical use, marketing, expenses, prices, and income. These data are released by the state offices in annual (and some quarterly) reports. Some data are reported for counties, others for multi-county crop reporting districts, and still others for states. Pertinent national data may also be included in the state reports. Table 11 shows how some of the NASS data are presented for Kossuth County.

NASS operates field offices in each state except Maine, New Hampshire, Vermont, Connecticut, Massachusetts, and Rhode Island (which are all part of a New England Regional office in Concord, New Hampshire). Questions about the state system should be referred to the Director, State Statistical Division, NASS, USDA South Building, Room 4143, 14th & Independence Ave. SW, Washington, DC 20250, or call (202) 720-3638.

The Economic Research Service (ERS) is the USDA agency responsible for analyzing and reporting much of the data collected by NASS, as well as agricultural and rural data from many other agencies and organizations. Most ERS analysis and research is done at the national and regional level. One exception is the November or December issue of *Economic Indicators of the Farm Sector.* It includes income and balance sheet accounts for each state based on the NASS Farm Costs and Returns Survey. Income accounts include net farm income, net cash income, net business income, net cash flow, cash income to farm operator households, and returns to operators from production transactions. Balance sheet accounts include the current market value of assets, debts, and net worth.

Table 11   State field offices of the National Agricultural Statistics Service publish annual production and marketing data.

	Kossuth County, Iowa (1992)		
Crop	Harvested for grain (acres)	Yield per acre (bushels)	Production (1,000 bu.)	Price received per bushel (dollars)
Corn	308,000	158.1	48,706	1.97
Soybeans	214,600	42.2	9,052	5.51
Oats	1,900	88.4	168	1.26

Source: Iowa Agricultural Statistics (8).

> ERS provides updated information on agriculture 24 hours a day. To access AutoFAX, call (202) 219-1107 from the touch-tone phone on a fax machine and wait for recorded instructions. The system will ask you for a document number and then send the document to your fax machine (up to three per call). Ask for document 0411 to get a list of directories available on the system, and ask for document 4001 for a directory of farm income documents. Each document is 3–6 pages in length. Among the available directories are guides to ERS information and data, specialty agriculture, national, and state farm income accounts, farm sector economics, and rural affairs.
>
> ERS data are also accessible through Internet (see Appendix F).

Up-to-date estimates of production, stocks, inventories, and other agricultural data are issued by USDA's Agricultural Statistics Board and the State Statistical Offices. For a free copy of the "Agricultural Statistics Board Catalog," write to ASB Publications, Room 5829, South Building, USDA, Washington, DC 20250, or call (202) 720-4020.

Forestry

The forestry industry includes timber production and harvest, forestry services (such as pest control and reforestation), and the manufacture of wood products.[10] Rural communities that depend on the forestry industry are scattered throughout the Pacific Northwest, upper Midwest, parts of the Southeast, and the extreme Northeast.

The issues facing the industry and communities that depend on forestry are complex, in part because so much forest land is Federally owned and therefore the focus of intense public scrutiny. Public policy must address questions about how to insure the long-term productivity of the nation's timber resources; preserve multiple uses of timber lands while protecting wildlife, soil, and water quality; and afford some measure of economic stability to the communities that depend on forestry. Some of the questions that people in such communities might ask include:

- How many local jobs and how much local income depend on forestry?

- Who owns the region's timber lands?

- How are regional timber resources being managed and used, and to whom are they being sold?

---

[10]The SIC system used by all Federal agencies includes logging and wood products (such as furniture, pulp, and paper) in the manufacturing industry. Some analysts, like Weber, Castle, and Shriver (48), include these related activities in the forestry industry. The latter convention is followed here.

- What is the size and structure of the forest products industry?
- How is local employment being affected by increased use of machinery, or alternatively, by the size of the timber harvest?

From the perspective of an individual community, data to answer questions like these are fragmented and difficult to find. (There is no census of forestry, for example.) Forestry is an industry whose level of income and employment is relatively minor in terms of the national economy but which is extremely important to some regions, especially in rural areas. Therefore, Federal statistics by themselves are insufficient for local analysis and must be supplemented by other data.

Researchers can start with the following:

- USDA's Forest Service, which is in charge of all Federally owned timber land;
- U.S. and state Forest and Range Experiment Stations, which conduct research on a variety of renewable resource issues; and
- state forestry agencies.

These sources can be supplemented with information from SESAs, *County Business Patterns*, and the Bureau of Economic Analysis.

One of the first questions that researchers might ask concerns the extent to which a community depends on the forestry industry for income and employment. At least a partial answer can be found in the environmental impact statement (EIS) developed by the Forest Service for every national forest. The EIS analyzes the direct and so-called "induced" effect of alternative forest management plans on the economy and physical environment of multicounty areas. For example, the EIS for White Mountain National Forest in northern New Hampshire evaluates how different harvest rates will affect income and employment in an area that includes Coos County and three adjacent counties (20).[11]

Researchers who are interested in data for a single county, or information about forestry dependence in areas where timber is privately held, must use more general secondary sources. With respect to employment data, SESAs collect information on wage and salary workers in the forestry industry including, for example, those who work in forestry services, and in lum-

---

[11]The Forest Service uses input–output analysis to describe the structural interdependencies in the regional economies affected by the agency's activities. With their "IMPLAN" model, they predict how various timberland management plans will affect local income and employment in areas that typically contain several counties. Robison and Freitag (13) have developed a technique to localize the IMPLAN model on a subcounty, community level.

ber and wood products manufacturing. The shortcomings of the SESA data are: (1) self-employed loggers and mill owners are not counted; (2) U.S. Forest Service workers are not reported separately from other Federal government workers; and (3) forestry workers employed for wages or salary are usually grouped with those in agriculture and fisheries.

One method to obtain this data is to try to get detailed wage and salary information directly from the SESA and then double-check these data with statistics from *County Business Patterns.* By combining the two sources (as well as data from private companies, if available), it may be possible to piece together a realistic employment profile for the forestry industry.

County-level income data for the forestry industry are even more problematic. BEA does not report either forestry proprietor or worker income separately. Researchers may be able to work with analysts in their state Forest and Range Experiment Station to develop independent estimates.

Another question that people in forestry-dependent communities might ask concerns the ownership and management of public and private timberland. National, regional, and local Forest Service offices can provide information about Federal ownership, while state and private forestry offices (located in the regional Forest Service offices), or individual state forestry agencies (where they exist) should be able to provide information about state-owned and private forest land.

Federal timber policy is guided by three Congressional acts that, in theory, provide public-sector forest managers with a framework for long-term planning. These managers are responsible for developing and implementing an

---

The U.S. Forest Service's Rural Community Assistance Program provides technical assistance and limited grant funds to eligible natural resource-based communities. The program helps communities that have been adversely affected by changes in natural resource policy with strategies to develop and diversify their economies. An important element of the program is that it works only on locally generated projects. For more information, contact the Forest Service in Washington, D.C. at (202) 205-1389.

The U.S. Forest Service publishes "A Guide to Your National Forests," which includes a map of all national forests, a directory of the nine regional and 123 local Forest Service offices, and a list of the eight Forest and Range Experiment Stations. The agency also publishes *Land Areas of the National Forest System,* a reference book that contains state-, county-, and Congressional district-level acreage data for national forests, wilderness areas, and other lands in the Forest Service system. Both publications can be ordered, free of charge, from the U.S. Forest Service, Public Affairs Office, P.O. Box 96090, Washington, DC, 20090-6090 or by calling (202) 205-0957.

official Forest Plan which is revised every 10 to 15 years. The Federal government uses the plans to communicate with the public. They set forth overall management principles and also specify targets for activities such as timber harvest, road construction, campground development, and protection of roadless areas. Forest Plans are available from local Forest Service offices.

The quality of information on the size and structure of the local forest products industry varies widely. Researchers should check with the regional Forest and Range Experiment Station and state forestry agency to find out what is available for their area.

Mining

The mining industry is a diverse sector that includes the extraction of minerals occurring naturally—solids such as coal and ores; liquids such as crude petroleum; and gases such as natural gas. The major factors that affect the industry's performance vary according to the particular substance that is mined, although in general, the industry is characterized by high instability. Mining-dependent counties, of which there are 146, are concentrated in Appalachia and scattered around the West.

The primary source of small-area data on the mining industry comes from the census of mineral industries, which covers all establishments with one or more paid employees. Information from this census allows us to answer questions about the local structure of the industry (how many establishments and employees), its payroll, value of shipments, and capital expenditures.

The enumeration method for the 1992 Census of Mineral Industries combined a mail questionnaire (for about 22,000 midsize and large establishments) with administrative record data from other Federal agencies (for about 11,500 smaller establishments). County data will be published in the Geographic Area Series of regional reports (MIC92-A), which is scheduled to be released in mid-1995. State-level data are available on CD-ROM, which will be updated quarterly and eventually include the county data as well. Table 12 shows how 1987 census data were published for Nicholas County.

Other small-area mining data are available from state agencies in those states where mining is an important activity. For example, the West Virginia Department of Mines issues an *Annual Report and Directory of Mines* which contains time series data on underground and surface mine coal production by county.

Staff from the Census Bureau's Services Division and Manufacturing and Construction Division handle data-related questions about trade, services, manufacturing, and mineral industries. See "Telephone Contacts, Bureau of the Census" or call Data User Services at (301) 457-4100 for names of subject-area specialists.

Table 12 Mining data come from the census of mineral industries.

Industry group[a]	Establishments		All employees		Production, development, and exploration workers		
	Total (number)	With 20 employees or more (number)	Number (thousands)	Payroll ($ million)	Number (thousands)	Hours (millions)	Wages ($ million)
Total	46	19	1.7	55.0	1.4	2.9	45.4
Bituminous coal and lignite mining	46	19	1.7	55.0	1.4	2.9	45.4

Nicholas County, West Virginia (1987)

[a]Data for the crude petroleum and natural gas and mining services industries were not collected by county in 1987.
Source: U.S. Department of Commerce, Bureau of the Census (40).

Manufacturing

Manufacturing-dependent counties, of which there are 506, are scattered throughout the eastern United States, with a few in the Northwest. One source of county-level data on the manufacturing industry is the census of manufactures, which covers all establishments "engaged in the mechanical or chemical transformation of materials or substances into new products" (39). Data from this census allow researchers to answer questions about the local structure of the industry, its payroll, cost of materials, value of its shipments exported out of the country, and new capital expenditures. County-level information is presented for the manufacturing industry as a whole, as well as for specific manufacturing industries that have at least 500 employees in a particular county.

Like the census of mineral industries, the enumeration method used for the 1992 census of manufactures combined a mail questionnaire (to about 200,000 midsize and large establishments) with administrative records (for about 150,000 single-establishment firms). Data for counties and selected places will be published in the Geographic Area Series (MC92-A) beginning in early 1995.

For larger-area statistics on the manufacturing industry, researchers can use state tables in the Geographic Area Series. For detailed statistics on divisions within the industry, researchers can consult the Industry Series (MC87-I). In the case of Coos County, where wood products are manufactured, for example, researchers would likely be interested in reports such as "Logging Camps, Sawmills, and Planing Mills" (Report 24A).

Because of the "500-employee" limit, the census of manufactures does not often provide detailed data in nonmetro counties. For Nicholas County, for example, the census provides data about establishments that manufacture "lumber and wood products," but not for the subcategories "logging" and "sawmills and planing mills." For more detail about manufacturing in Coos County, researchers can use data from *County Business Patterns* (*CBP*), which are illustrated in Table 13. Among other things, *CBP* data indicate that

The Energy Information Administration (EIA) collects and publishes output, employment, and productivity data on the coal, petroleum, natural gas, and other energy industries. Researchers can order a free copy of the annual *EIA Publications Directory,* the quarterly *EIA Directory of Electronic Products,* and the bimonthly bulletin, "New Releases." Call (202) 586-8800, or write the National Energy Information Center, EI-231, Room 1F-048, Forrestal Building, Washington, DC 20585. EIA is also accessible via Internet e-mail (*INFOCTR@EIA.DOE.GOV*).

Table 13 *County Business Patterns* adds some detail to economic censuses like the census of manufactures.

Industry	Total number of establishments	Coos County, New Hampshire (1992) Number of employees for week including March 12[a]	Annual payroll ($1,000)[b]
Lumber and wood products	66	483	8,767
Logging	52	267	4,309
Sawmills and planing mills	9	193	4,125
Furniture and fixtures	2	(a)	(D)
Household furniture	2	(a)	(D)
Paper and allied products	5	(b)	(D)
Paper mills	2	(b)	(D)
Miscellaneous converted paper products	3	(c)	(D)

[a](a) 100–249 employees; (b) 1,000–2,499 employees; (c) 250–499 employees.
[b](D) Withheld to avoid disclosing data for individual establishments.
Source: U.S. Department of Commerce, Bureau of the Census (30).

"logging" makes up 55 percent of "lumber and wood products employment," but only 49 percent of the payroll.

Trade

The trade industry includes firms that sell merchandise either to other firms (wholesale trade) or to consumers (retail trade).

The primary sources of small-area data on the trade industry are the censuses of retail and wholesale trade. Like others in the economic series, the trade censuses allow us to answer questions about numbers of establishments and employees, payroll, and value of sales. In the case of retail trade, these statistics are provided for ten types of industries for counties and places that have at least 350 establishments with paid employees. Less detail is available from the census of wholesale trade, which provides statistics for only two kinds of establishments—merchant wholesalers (which own the goods they sell) and "other operating types" (which act as agents and do not actually own what they sell).

The enumeration method for the 1992 trade censuses combined a mail questionnaire (for midsize and larger establishments) with administrative records (for smaller establishments). Data for counties and places with at least 2,500 population will be published in the Geographic Area Series (RC92-A and WC92-A), which is being released as this book goes to press.

Publications based on the census of retail trade report the number of establishments and total sales for ten kinds of retail businesses, such as food stores, eating and drinking places, and apparel and accessory stores.

Other small-area retail trade data are available from a private source called the *Annual Survey of Buying Power* issued by Sales and Marketing Management. Published annually within 12 months of the reference year, *Survey of Buying Power* includes retail sales estimates by selected SIC groups, including establishments that sell food; eating and drinking places; general merchandise stores; furniture, furnishing, and appliance stores; automotive supply stores; and drug stores. Sales and Marketing Management uses census of retail trade data as benchmarks, and then uses other public and private sources to update the census data.

Two other reference books that yield small-area (marketing) data are *The Sourcebook of County Demographics,* and *The Sourcebook of Zip Code Demographics,* published by CACI Marketing Systems, a private firm. For counties and zip codes, both books contain data on population, age, race, household income, purchasing trends, and also have business data for the 2-digit SIC level on total number of firms and employees. These data come from the census, Current Population Survey, other agency data, and private marketing surveys. Both books are also available on CD-ROM, but are quite expensive. Check your nearest depository library or call CACI at (800) 292-2224.

The Census Bureau issues monthly and annual current trade statistics for the United States and, in some cases, states and regions. See the *Census Catalog and Guide* or call Data User Services at (301) 457-4100 for more information.

Services
The service industry includes establishments that provide services to individuals, businesses, and governments. Examples of service establishments are hotels; personal service businesses such as laundries and barber shops; business service companies that do advertising or data processing, for example; health, legal, and educational services; and private households that employ workers in domestic service. Some people confuse the service industry with the service sector. The "sector" is a broader classification which includes all industries producing no tangible product—such as transportation, communications, trade, household services, and government.

Many rural communities see the service industry as a possible vehicle for economic development. Some service-based strategies focus on attracting tourists, while others concentrate on retirees (who may need health care,

Table 14 The census of service industries provides data on industries that are becoming more important to some rural communities.

Establishments with payroll in selected kind-of-business groups (1992)[a]

	Hotels, motels, and other lodging places		Automotive repair, services, and garages		Amusement and recreation services		Health services		Legal services	
	Number	Payroll ($1,000)	Number	Payroll ($1,000)	Number	Payroll ($1,000)	Number	Payroll ($1,000)	Number	Payroll ($1,000)
Yavapai County, AZ	60	36,629	92	17,354	50	18,168	221	85,596	57	11,324
Camp Verde	1	(D)	4	657	—	—	6	3,680	1	(D)
Chino Valley	—	—	2	(D)	—	—	2	(D)	1	(D)
Cottonwood	7	2,881	7	1,275	6	1,851	30	10,522	6	(D)
Prescott	20	(D)	46	9,804	12	6,351	130	58,663	37	9,146
Prescott Valley	2	(D)	6	1,067	2	(D)	11	2,422	1	(D)
Sedona (part)	2	(D)	—	—	1	(D)	1	(D)	—	—
Balance of county[b]	28	17,446	27	(D)	29	9,111	41	9,489	11	1,360

[a](D) Withheld to avoid disclosing data for individual companies.

[b]Balance of county includes places with population less than 2,500.

Source: U.S. Department of Commerce, Bureau of the Census (43).

nursing homes, and other services). Critics of such strategies warn that parts of the service industry are unstable because they are sensitive to changes in consumer income and that jobs generated by the industry are often unskilled, seasonal, and low wage.

The primary source of small-area data about this industry is the census of service industries, which covers most service establishments except education; labor, political, and religious organizations; and private households. Data for this census are gathered primarily through a mail questionnaire and from administrative records (for the smallest establishments).

Statistics from the census of service industries include numbers of establishments and employees, payroll, and receipts. The data are provided by specific type of business for counties and places with 350 or more service establishments with paid employees. Table 14 shows how the data were presented for Yavapai County in 1992. (As in the case of manufacturing statistics, data for divisions within the industry are available in *CBP*.)

Other data for selected service industries may be available from state commerce or business development agencies. In particular, states that actively promote tourism typically collect information on lodging places, restaurants, and recreation services.

The Role of the Federal Government

Although the Federal government provides a relatively small share of local government revenue (see Chapter 5), it does make a substantial contribution to local economies by transferring income and making loans directly to individuals and businesses. Researchers can learn the size of that contribution by using the *Consolidated Federal Funds Report* (*CFFR*), an annual Census Bureau publication that contains small-area data on Federal government expenditures and obligations.

Statistics in the two-volume *CFFR* are up to date because the publication is issued approximately six months after the fiscal year to which it pertains (October 1 to September 30). Volume 1 covers county areas and includes statistics on grants to local governments, salaries and wages, procurement contracts (defense and other), direct payments to individuals (retirement and disability, and other), loans (direct and guaranteed), and some other major programs. Volume 2 covers subcounty areas and includes statistics on grants to local governments, procurement contracts (defense and other), and loans (direct and guaranteed). All of the *CFFR* data are available electronically. Data for a ten-year period are on CD-ROM for county areas.

Figure 18 illustrates *CFFR* data for Yavapai and Kossuth counties. On a per capita basis, Kossuth receives almost twice as much money from the Federal government (including direct payments as well as loans and guaran-

Figure 18 The *Consolidated Federal Funds Report* enables researchers to track the geographic distribution of Federal money.

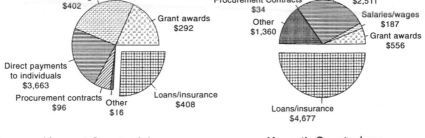

Government Funds Per Capita (1993)

Salaries/wages $402
Grant awards $292
Direct payments to individuals $3,663
Procurement contracts $96
Other $16
Loans/insurance $408

Yavapai County, Arizona

Procurement Contracts $34
Other $1,360
Direct payments to individuals $2,511
Salaries/wages $187
Grant awards $556
Loans/insurance $4,677

Kossuth County, Iowa

Source. U.S. Department of Commerce, Bureau of Census (28).

tees) as Yavapai. The difference is due primarily to direct loans and guaranteed loans and insurance, most likely issued to local farmers. Because of its high concentration of retirees, Yavapai County receives a relatively larger share of direct payments to individuals, which include retirement and disability programs.

5

Analyzing Government in Rural Communities

Many state and local governments around the country are under severe financial stress. One reason is that as Federal aid has decreased relative to personal income, the number and scope of top-down, unfunded mandates have increased. These mandates cover a variety of social services, public transportation, environmental issues, and other responsibilities. They are public sector obligations defined at the national level, even though financial and administrative responsibility for carrying them out resides at the state and local level (5).

Unfortunately, many state and local governments are ill equipped to deal with these new and growing responsibilities. Lower levels of governments have been unwilling, and often unable, to raise the revenue needed to carry out obligations from the national level (15). Since increased Federal assistance is unlikely, many communities face politically difficult choices between raising tax revenues, cutting services, or finding ways to provide services at a lower cost. Making these choices in an informed way requires a thorough understanding of local government structure and of how various government units generate revenue and spend money. Some of the specific questions that a researcher might ask are:

- How many and what kind of jurisdictions exist in the locality, what services do they provide, and which ones are authorized to levy taxes and spend money?

- What percentage of local revenue comes from intergovernmental transfers (Federal and state), and from *own sources,* which is raised by the government unit itself (e.g., property taxes, and sales taxes)?

- How are these revenues used to provide various services?

- How do expenditures and service levels compare with state, regional, or national norms?

- How many people are employed by the local government and how much do they earn?

In addition to reports from the census of governments, the Census Bureau publishes reports based on annual and quarterly surveys on such topics as government employment, finance, and public employee retirement systems. Many of these reports include data for individual government units. See the most recent *Census Catalog and Guide* for more information. Two brochures, "Current Government Reports" and "1992 Census of Governments," are also useful guides. To order, write to the Chief of Governments Division, Bureau of the Census, Washington, DC 20233.

In general, all census of governments data and associated annual surveys covering government finances and employment are available by the individual government unit. The data are not restricted by confidentiality. While the numbers are not usually released in printed format, they are available from data files contained on magnetic tape as well as other formats. The Census Bureau is now releasing data via Internet, although currently these data are limited to large government units and state summaries of local governments. Contact your state data center or regional Census office to find out if unpublished data are available for your area.

The most useful and easy-to-find statistics for answering these kinds of questions are issued by the Census Bureau. These statistics come from the census of governments, which is conducted in years ending in "2" and "7." The reports in the government series include data on some 85,000 local units of government below the Federal and state levels, including counties, municipalities, townships, school districts, and special districts.

A word of caution before we discuss how researchers can use these statistics: Analyzing local government is very complicated. Often, published data are not comparable across areas because budgeting and accounting practices differ from state to state and from one jurisdiction to another within a state. Therefore, we strongly recommend that if you want to research local government issues, consult first with local planners, people who are responsible for budgeting and accounting within the local jurisdiction, or other knowledgeable people.

Local Government Structure

Researchers can answer questions about the structure of local governments with information from the Census Bureau report called *Government Organization,* Series GC(1)-1. The most up-to-date edition of this report is based on data from the 1992 census of governments. It provides information

Table 15 *Government Organization,* a report from the census of governments, is
a primer on local governments and public school systems.

| | Number of governmental units (1992) | | | | |
| | | | | Special district | |
County	Total[a]	Municipal	School district	Total	With property taxing power
Attala, MS	10	4	2	3	—
Coos, NH	44	1	16	7	3
Kossuth, IA	21	12	7	1	—
Latah, ID	40	9	5	25	24
Nicholas, WV	12	2	1	8	—
Yavapai, AZ	53	8	23	21	21

[a]Includes county government as a separate unit. Coos County total includes 19 township
units.
Source: U.S. Department of Commerce, Bureau of the Census (35).

on the number and selected characteristics of local government units and
public school systems as of the beginning of 1992. County-level data items
are: (1) number of local governmental units and (2) type of units (municipal,
township, school district, and special district).

Data for our sample counties from the 1992 *Government Organization*
report are illustrated in Table 15. As the table shows, Coos County has 44
separate government units, compared to only ten in Attala County.

For every state, *Government Organization* describes each type of government unit and school system in terms of its purpose, authorizing legislation,
and funding source. For example, we learn from the report that in Idaho,
there are 22 separate types of governments. Among these are "special districts," which include such entities as port districts, housing authorities, fire
protection districts in unincorporated areas, weed districts, and intercounty
rural library districts.

Local Government Finance

After learning how local government is structured, a researcher might want
to know where public revenues come from and how they are spent. As we
mentioned above, budgeting and accounting practices differ from place to
place, so it is important to consult with knowledgeable people before tack-
ling this subject.

The Census Bureau reports revenue and expenditure data for counties in
the *Compendium of Government Finances,* one of five reports in Series

GC(4). (As this book goes to press, the 1992 edition has not yet been released.) Revenues are classified by type: intergovernmental, general from own sources, and utility and liquor store. Expenditures are classified by function: education services, social service and income maintenance, transportation, public safety, environment and housing, government administration, and utilities.

Figure 19 illustrates how a researcher might use these revenue data. For all six sample counties, revenue from the Federal government paid directly to the county government makes up a very small share of total revenue. Coos County gets the largest share from the Federal government, probably because so much of the county is made up of Forest Service land.

Another report in Series GC(4), *Finances of County Governments* GC (4)-3, contains information on revenue, expenditure, debt, and assets for individual county governments. It also contains national and population size-groups to allow comparison of data. Other reports in the series present

Figure 19   The *Compendium of Government Finances* provides data on local government revenue.

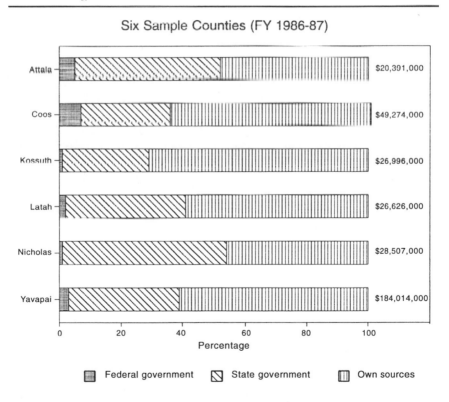

Six Sample Counties (FY 1986-87)

Attala	$20,391,000
Coos	$49,274,000
Kossuth	$26,996,000
Latah	$26,626,000
Nicholas	$28,507,000
Yavapai	$184,014,000

0   20   40   60   80   100
Percentage

■ Federal government   ◨ State government   ▥ Own sources

Source: U.S. Department of Commerce, Bureau of the Census (26).

larger-area data on government revenues, by source and type; expenditures, by function, character, and object; indebtedness and debt transactions; and cash and security holdings.

Own source revenue comes from two sources. The first consists of taxes, such as real property, personal property, income, and sales. The second is made up of charges and miscellaneous revenues, such as interest earnings, fees and permit revenue, and user fees for water, solid waste disposal, and recreation.

One very important component of own source revenue is the property tax. When property tax revenues fluctuate from year to year (as they do in some resource-based rural communities), providing public services that depend on property taxes is especially difficult. For example, between 1982 and 1986, plummeting land values in many farm-dependent communities caused property tax collections to decline. This placed severe stress on the ability of local governments to finance education and other public services (19).

One source of data for analyzing local property tax values is the Census Bureau report called *Taxable Property Values,* Series GC(2). It contains information on assessed valuations, property sales, and property tax rates. County-level data items are: (1) gross assessed property value (total, real, and personal); (2) the tax-exempt portion of locally assessed value (real and personal); and (3) assessed value subject to tax (total, state assessed, and locally assessed). Like other reports in this series, the most recent edition is based on data from the 1992 census of governments.

Because local governments must make budget projections annually or biannually, it is often important for officials to know how the property tax base is changing from year to year. Census data are issued only every five years, so people who need more up-to-date information should contact their county tax assessor. Although property values are a matter of public record, assessors vary in how accessible they make the data. In some states, funding provides incentives for communities to assess property at less than fair market value. Where these incentives are large, people may get more accurate information about local property values from the State Department of Revenue or State Board of Equalization than from local officials.

Just as important as knowing where the money comes from is knowing how it is spent. Again using the *Compendium of Government Finances,* researchers can learn how much their local government spends on various public services, and how their expenditures compare to those made in other communities. Expenditure categories include education, social services and income maintenance, transportation, public safety, and environment and housing. For example, Figure 20 shows per capita expenditures on police protection by each of the six sample counties. In 1987, Yavapai County spent the most and Nicholas County spent the least.

Other tables in this Census report show each state's revenue and expendi-

Figure 20   The *Compendium of Government Finances* also provides data on
local government expenditures.

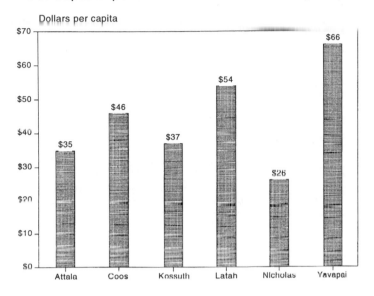

Per Capita Expenditures on Police Protection (1987)

Dollars per capita

Source: U.S. Department of Commerce, Bureau of the Census (26).

ture data for groups of counties of similar population size. There are eight
population-size groups ranging from "less than 10,000" to "1,000,000 or
more." With this information, researchers can compare their county budget
to that of counties with roughly the same number of people. They might, for
example, learn that there are economies of scale for certain services; that is,
the cost of providing a particular service might be less for larger counties. If
this is the case, two counties might be able to save money if they offer the
service jointly instead of individually. Alternatively, the cost of providing
services might be affected by population density rather than size, a relationship that the Census Bureau data would not reveal.

Public Employment

Public employee payroll is one of the largest components of local government expenditures and is, therefore, often a target for budget cuts. Using
Census Bureau data, researchers can find out how many people are employed

to provide public services in their county. They can also compare their public employment and payroll levels to those in counties of similar size around
the United States.

The source of such information is a report called *Public Employment,*
Series GC(3). One of the volumes in this report, *Compendium of Public
Employment,* includes county-level data on number of employees by function, as well as October earnings for full-time teachers and all other public
employees.

Figure 21 illustrates how these data can be used. Of the six sample counties, local government hired the most full-time equivalent (FTE) teachers per
1,000 population in Nicholas County, and the least in Kossuth County. In
October 1987, these teachers earned the highest salary in Yavapai County and
the lowest salary in Attala County.

Figure 21   The *Compendium of Public Employment* provides data on public service employees and earnings.

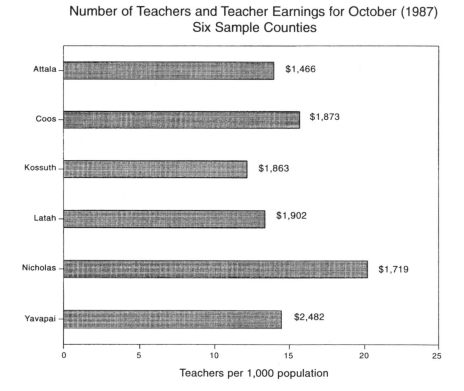

Number of Teachers and Teacher Earnings for October (1987)
Six Sample Counties

Source: U.S. Department of Commerce, Bureau of the Census (27).

Again, the Census Bureau issues these data only once every five years, so people who need more up-to-date data should contact local agencies, such as their county or municipal government office.

In between census of governments reports (issued every five years) are several annual Current Government Reports that can help researchers compare data for different governments. *Public Employment* (GE-1) gives national totals on October employment and payrolls of all governments, by function and type, and local government employment and payroll, by function. *City Employment* (GE-2) provides national and population-size group statistics on October employment and payrolls of municipal governments, by function. *County Government Employment* (GE-4) provides national and population-size group statistics on October employment and payrolls of county governments, by function, and gives comparable data for previous years.

Glossary

For more detail, readers are encouraged to refer to original sources referenced in the text.

administrative data Data collected in the course of an organization's normal business; for example, the Internal Revenue Service's file of all income tax returns.

age pyramid A bar graph that shows the age distribution of a population. Age pyramids are usually constructed using five-year intervals, with the older age intervals at the top of the graph.

aggregate income See *total personal income.*

Beale coding system Classifies all U.S. counties into ten groups based on urban/rural population characteristics and location with respect to urban areas. Includes six groups of nonmetro counties and four groups of metro counties. Also referred to as the "Urban-Rural Continuum Code."

block The Census Bureau term for a small geographic area with discernable boundaries but no minimum population. Blocks are the smallest geographic units used by the Census Bureau for collecting and reporting data. In rural areas, block boundaries may be visible features such as roads, powerlines, fences, and abandoned railroads.

census A count, or enumeration, of the population.

census county division (CCD) A county subdivision designated by the Census Bureau for statistical purposes in states where *minor civil divisions* do not exist.

census designated place (CDP) The Census Bureau term for an unincorporated, closely settled population center with at least 1,000 inhabitants and without legally established boundaries. CDPs are designated for statistical purposes.

constant dollars See *real dollars.*

consumer price index (CPI) A single number which gives the average value of current consumer prices compared to some base period. Compiled by the Bureau of Labor Statistics, the CPI measures how much inflation (or deflation) is occurring across the entire range of consumer goods.

current dollars Dollars that have not been adjusted by a price index (such as the *consumer price index*), as contrasted with *real dollars*.

decennial census A *census* taken every ten years. The U.S. Census Bureau conducts a decennial census of population and housing in years ending in "0" (zero).

demography A science concerned with the size, geographic distribution, structure, and change of human populations. Demographic statistics include those that pertain to the sex and age composition, mortality and fertility, educational and economic characteristics, and migration of a population.

enumeration district The Census Bureau term for a geographical area assigned to one *enumerator.*

enumeration method The method by which data are collected, for example, with a mail questionnaire, personal interview, or from administrative records.

enumerator In the case of the decennial census, a Census Bureau employee who is hired to count housing units and personally interview a sample of the population. More generally, a person who conducts interviews.

environmental impact statement (EIS) In the case of the U.S. Forest Service, an analysis of the direct and indirect effects of alternative forest management plans on the economy and physical environment of a multi-county area. More generally, an analysis of how a particular development project will affect resource use and quality in a local area.

establishment A business or industrial unit at a single physical location that produces or distributes goods or performs services, for example, a single store or factory.

industry Kind of establishment; an establishment's economic activity, such as agriculture, medical services, construction, or retail trade.

intercensal Between the years of the *decennial census.* Working with state agencies, the Census Bureau makes intercensal estimates of the population of all U.S. counties and subcounty governmental units.

labor and proprietor income (LPI) One component of *personal income* estimates from the Bureau of Economic Analysis. Includes (1) wages and salaries paid to employees, (2) other labor income consisting primarily of employer contributions to private pension and welfare funds, and (3) income to self-employed individuals (proprietors), partnerships, and tax-exempt cooperatives.

labor force The part of the population that is employed or available for work. The labor force includes people who are in the armed forces, employed, unemployed, or actively seeking employment. The Census Bureau currently publishes labor force statistics for persons age 16 years and older.

labor force participation rate Proportion of people age 16 years and older who are in the *labor force;* that is, the number of people who are employed or available for work divided by the number of people who are age 16 years and older.

longitudinal study A study that involves data collection from the same respondents at different points in time. For example, in a longitudinal study in Wisconsin, researchers interviewed a sample of farmers in 1982 and again in 1987 to learn how the respondents adjusted to major changes in the agricultural economy.

mean family income The average amount of income received by each family, that is, total income divided by the number of families.

median income The income level at which half of the population have lower incomes and half have higher incomes; the middle income level.

metropolitan (metro) county The Census Bureau term for any county in a *metropolitan statistical area.*

metropolitan statistical area (MSA) An area designated by the Census that is made up of one or more counties around a large population center, together with adjacent communities that are socially and economically integrated with the central county. An MSA must either have (1) a city with a population of at least 50,000 or (2) an urbanized area (which is a *census designated place)* with a population of at least 50,000 and a total MSA population of at least 100,000.

minor civil division (MCD) The Census Bureau term for a governmental unit that is smaller than a county, such as a town or township.

money income Term used by the Census Bureau for cash income such as wages and salaries, interest, rental income, Social Security payments, and public assistance.

natural increase The difference between the number of births and deaths in a particular area. Together, natural increase and *net migration* are responsible for population change. (In rare instances, deaths outnumber births, resulting in natural decrease.)

net migration The difference between the number of people who move into an area (in-migrants) and the number who move out (out-migrants).

If in-migrants outnumber out-migrants, the area experiences net in-migration and vice versa.

nonmetropolitan (nonmetro) county A county that is not part of a Census Bureau–designated *metropolitan statistical area*.

occupation Kind of work; a person's activity on the job either for pay or profit, such as farmer, nurse, computer programmer, bus driver, or logger.

per capita income The mean or average income received by individuals; that is, *total personal income* divided by the total number of people.

personal income A measure of income used by the Bureau of Economic Analysis, defined as the income received by, or on behalf of, residents of a particular area. Includes *labor and proprietor income* less contributions for social insurance programs such as Social Security; dividends, interest, and rent; and transfer payments.

poverty level or **threshold** An income level below which a family, household, or individual is officially considered to be poor. Each year, the U.S. Office of Management and Budget establishes a series of poverty income levels for different family sizes and ages of household heads. For example, in 1993, the poverty level for a family of four was $14,763.

poverty rate The proportion of people living below the *poverty level*; that is, the number of people (individuals, families, or households) who have incomes less than the poverty level divided by the total population.

primary data Data collected by a researcher for a specific study using personal or telephone interviews, for example.

proprietor income A term used by the Bureau of Economic Analysis to refer to income received by proprietors (self-employed persons), persons in business partnerships, and members of tax-exempt cooperatives.

quintile A group that makes up one-fifth of the distribution of a given population. With respect to income, the lowest quintile of families has the characteristic that four-fifths of all other families in the population have higher incomes.

real dollars *Current dollars* that have been adjusted by the *consumer price index* to reflect changes in inflation (or deflation). Economists adjust current dollars so they can measure the dollars' value in terms of the goods and services that can be purchased. Hence, 1989 income measured in real terms, for example, can be compared to 1970 income because the effect of inflation has been removed. *Current dollars* divided by the *consumer price index* equal *real dollars*.

rural A term used to describe all persons (or areas) that are not designated by the Census Bureau as *urban.*

sample design The method used to select a sample of elements from a given population for purposes of analysis. Examples of sample designs are (1) *random sampling,* where a scientifically generated table of random numbers is used to select elements, and (2) *systematic sampling,* where every *k*th (for example, every 10th or 50th) element of the population is selected for analysis.

sampling rate or **ratio** The proportion of elements in a population that are selected for analysis.

secondary data Existing data that have already been collected and transferred to hard copy, microfiche, or a computer accessible format. Examples of secondary data sources are the *County and City Data Book* and reports from the decennial census.

service industry Includes establishments that provide services to individuals, businesses, and governments. These are personal services; private household services; miscellaneous business and repair services; amusement and recreation services; professional, social, and related services; and hotels and other lodging places.

service sector Includes all industries that produce no tangible product, such as transportation, communications, trade, establishments in the *service industry,* and government.

standard industrial classification (SIC) system The Federal government's method of grouping businesses and other establishments by the type of economic activity in which they are engaged.

survey data Data collected with a questionnaire for specific research rather than in the course of an organization's normal business. For example, decennial census data are survey data.

time series data Observations on the same unit (for example, on the per acre price of Iowa cropland or on median household income) at two or more (usually many) points in time.

total personal income BEA's summary income measure that includes all income received by persons in a given area, including earnings, property income, and *transfer payments.*

transfer payments Income received not in return for current services—for example, Unemployment Insurance, Social Security, Aid to Families with Dependent Children, and Medicare.

unearned income Income from the ownership of property and other assets (that is, dividends, interest, and rent) plus *transfer payments*.

urban Term used by the Census Bureau to describe the population of all persons living in *urbanized areas* as well as persons living in places of 2,500 or more inhabitants outside urbanized areas.

urbanized area Central cities and surrounding densely settled territory with a combined population of at least 50,000 inhabitants.

wage and salary income Income earned at a job. The "labor" component of *labor and proprietor income*.

Appendices

Appendix A Selected Data Series from the Bureau of the Census, U.S. Department of Commerce

Series and/or Title	Description	Frequency	Format[a]	Comments
POPULATION, CENSUS Summary Pop. and Housing Char. (CPH-1) Pop. and Housing Unit Counts (CPH-2) Summary Soc., Econ., and Housing Char. (CPH-5) General Pop. Char. (CP-1) Soc. and Econ. Char. (CP-2)	Complete count and/or sample of items including demographic characteristics, Hispanic origin, education and labor force status, income by type and poverty status, urban/rural and metro/nonmetro breaks. Please see *Census Catalog and Guide 1994*, p. 220 for more detail.	Years ending in "0"	Published, fiche, CD-ROM (CPH-2 and CPH-5 only published)	CPH-1, CPH-2 and CP-1 are available for MCDs, CCDs, county subdivisions, places, and AI/ANAs. CPH-5 is available for local governmental units (counties, incorporated places) and AI/ANAs. CP-2 is available for places with population of 2,500 or more. Easy to use and available in local libraries.
HOUSING, CENSUS General Housing Char. (CH-1)	Complete count of items including number of units, number of rooms and occupants, and value. Urban/rural and metro/nonmetro breaks.	Years ending in "0"	Published, fiche, CD-ROM	Data for county subdivisions—places with at least 1,000 population and state parts of AI/ANAs. Frequently available in public libraries.

POPULATION, CURRENT PROGRAMS Population Characteristics,[b] P-20	Marital status, household, and family characteristics (including rural and farm families), mobility, fertility, educational attainment, etc. Some metro/nonmetro classifications.	Annual	Published, fiche, online	Geographic detail below national level varies. Farm detail only to regions.
Special Studies,[b] P-23	Various subjects, including migration, family, women, older people, metro/nonmetro residents.	Irregular	Published, fiche, online	Geographic detail below national level varies.
Local Population Estimates, P-25 and PPL	Estimates of population and components of change.	Irregular	Published (being phased out), photocopy of printed tables upon request, online, diskette	Estimates are made for counties and, in some cases, subcounty areas. Prepared jointly by state agencies and Census Bureau. Reliability of small place estimates is questionable.
Consumer Income,[b] P-60	Money income, noncash benefits, and poverty status by demographic characteristics. Some metro/nonmetro classifications.	Annual	Published, fiche, online	National and regional, some state.

Continued

Appendix A *Continued*

Series and/or Title	Description	Frequency	Format[a]	Comments
AGRICULTURE, CENSUS Geographic Area Series (AC-A)	Number and characteristics of farms and farm operators, land in farms, value of products sold, etc.	Years ending in "2" and "7"	Published, fiche, online, CD-ROM	Data are available at county level.
RETAIL TRADE, CENSUS Geographic Area Series (RC-A)	Number of establishments, employment, payroll, sales, etc., by various retail classifications.	Years ending in "2" and "7"	Published, fiche, online, CD-ROM	Counties and cities with 350+ establishments; counties and cities with 2,500+ population.
WHOLESALE TRADE, CENSUS Geographic Area Series (WC-A)	Number of establishments, employment, payroll, sales, etc.	Years ending in "2" and "7"	Published, fiche, online, CD-ROM	Counties and cities with 200+ establishments; counties and cities with 2,500+ population.
SERVICE INDUSTRIES, CENSUS Geographic Area Series (SC-A)	Number of establishments, receipts, payroll, and employment by type of business.	Years ending in "2" and "7"	Published, fiche, online, CD-ROM	Counties and cities with 350+ establishments; counties and cities with 2,500+ population.

	Content	Frequency	Format	Geographic coverage
MINERAL INDUSTRIES, CENSUS Geographic Area Series (MIC-A)	Number of establishments, value added by mining, employment, payroll, hours worked etc., by SIC.	Years ending in "2" and "7"	Published, fiche, online	Counties
MANUFACTURES, CENSUS Geographic Area Series (MC-A)	Number of establishments, employment, production workers and hours, payroll for all and production workers, expenses, capital expenditures, value added, and receipts for establishments with payroll.	Years ending in "2" and "7"	Published, CD-ROM	Counties and places with 2,500+ population. Number of establishments to zip code level.
COUNTY BUSINESS PATTERNS	Number of employees in mid-March pay period, total payrolls, number and employment size, class of establishments by 4-digit SIC, county.	Annual	Published, fiche, online, CD-ROM	Counties. Excludes farm and some other workers, also farmers and other self-employed. Federal employment and payroll only for hospitals and liquor stores. Data suppressed at county level for SIC codes with fewer than 50 employees.

Continued

Appendix A   *Continued*

Series and/or Title	Description	Frequency	Format[a]	Comments
GOVERNMENTS, CENSUS Government Organization (GC (1))	Local governments by type, size, and population; school systems by enrollment, etc.	Years ending in "2" and "7"	Published, fiche, online, CD-ROM	Counties, municipalities, townships, school districts, special districts. Description of local government structure in each state.
Taxable Property Values (GC (2))	Assessed valuations, measurable sales, number of properties, etc.	Years ending in "2" and "7"	Published, fiche, online, CD-ROM	Counties and cities of 50,000+ population.
Public Employment (GC (3))	Public employees, payrolls, October earnings, employment by function, etc.	Years ending in "2" and "7"	Published, fiche, online, CD-ROM	Type of government, states, counties, municipalities.
Government Finances (GC (4))	Revenue by source and type, expenditures, debt information, etc.	Years ending in "2" and "7"	Published, fiche, online, CD-ROM	Type of government, U.S., states, counties.
GOVERNMENTS, SURVEY Government Employment (GE)	Employment and payroll.	Annual	Published, fiche, online	By size classification of counties, cities, townships.

Government Finances (GF)	Federal, state, and local finances.	Annual	Published, fiche, online	By size classification of counties and selected sub-county areas.
Quarterly Summary of Federal, State, and Local Tax Revenue (GT)	Revenue by level of government and type of tax, county property tax collections.	Quarterly	Published, fiche, online	States, and by size classification of counties.
Consolidated Federal Funds Report	Grants, salaries and wages, procurement contracts, direct payments to individuals, other major programs.	Fiscal year	Published, fiche, online	Counties, municipalities, and townships (incorporated places only).
COUNTY AND CITY DATA BOOK	Statistical abstract supplement; data compiled from censuses, other agencies, and private sources. Population totals, income, education, etc.	Periodic	Published, online, diskette, CD-ROM	Counties, incorporated places with 25,000+ population and places with 2,500+ population.

Continued

Appendix A *Continued*

Series and/or Title	Description	Frequency	Format[a]	Comments
USA COUNTIES	Statistical abstract supplement, useful for time-series analysis; data compiled from censuses, other agencies, and private sources. Population figures from 1970–1992, sample data from 1990 census, economic census data.	Annual	CD-ROM	Counties

[a]May also be issued on tape.
[b]From Current Population Survey.
Source: U.S. Department of Commerce, Bureau of the Census (23).

Appendix B Selected Items Collected and Published in the 1992 Economic Censuses for Counties[a]

Item	Retail Trade	Wholesale Trade	Service Industries	Manufactures	Mineral Industries
Number of Establishments and Firms					
• Establishments with payroll	•	•	•	•	•
• Establishments without payroll[b]	•[c]	•	•[c]		
Employment					
• All employees	•	•	•	•	•
• Production workers/hours				•	•
• Employment size of establishments	•[d]		•[d]		•
Payroll					
• All employees, entire year	•	•	•	•	•
• All employees, first quarter	•	•	•		
• Production workers				•	•
Sales, Receipts, or Value of Shipments					
• For establishments with payroll	•	•	•	•	•
• For establishments without payroll[b]	•		•		
Other					
• Value added				•	•

[a]Some data are also available for places with 2,500 inhabitants or more and by zip code.
[b]Businesses which do not employ any workers.
[c]County and place data available only in computerized media.
[d]Subnational data available only in computerized media.

Source: U.S. Department of Commerce, Bureau of the Census (39).

Appendix C   Regional Rural Development Centers

North Central Regional Center for Rural Development
216 East Hall
Iowa State University
Ames, IA 50011-1070
Director: Cornelia B. Flora
(515) 294-8321

Southern Rural Development Center
Mississippi State University
P.O. Box 9656
Mississippi State, MS 39762-9656
Director: Doss Broadnax
(601) 325-3207

Northeast Regional Center for Rural Development
7 Armsby Building
Pennsylvania State University
University Park, PA 16802-5600
Director: Daryl Heasley
(814) 863-4656

Western Rural Development Center
Ballard Extension Hall 307
Oregon State University
Corvallis, OR 97331-3607
Director: Russ Youmans
(503) 737-3621

Appendix D Depository Libraries, State Data Centers, and BLS Cooperating Agencies

State or Territory	Federal Depository Library[a]	State Data Center	BLS Cooperating State Agency
Alabama	Auburn University Montgomery Library Montgomery	Alabama State Data Center Center for Business & Economic Research University of Alabama Tuscaloosa (205) 348-6191	Labor Market Information Dept. of Industrial Relations Montgomery (205) 242-8855
Alaska	Alaska State Library Juneau	State Data Center Dept. of Labor, Research & Analysis Juneau (907) 465-6026	Research and Analysis Alaska Department of Labor Juneau (907) 465-4500
Arizona	Dept. of Library Archives & Public Records Phoenix	Arizona Department of Security Phoenix (602) 542-5984	Labor Market Information Dept. of Economic Security Phoenix (602) 542-3871
Arkansas	Arkansas State Library Little Rock	State Data Center University of Arkansas—Little Rock Little Rock (501) 569-8530	Technical Support Employment Security Division Little Rock (501) 682-1543

Continued

Appendix D   *Continued*

State or Territory	Federal Depository Library[a]	State Data Center	BLS Cooperating State Agency
California	California State Library Sacramento	State Census Data Center Department of Finance Sacramento (916) 322-4651	Employment Development Dept. Employment Data & Research Division Sacramento (916) 427-4657
Colorado	Denver Public Library Denver	Colorado Department of Local Affairs Division of Local Government Denver (303) 866-2156	Labor Market Information Colorado Dept. of Labor & Employment Denver (303) 937-4947
Connecticut	Connecticut State Library Hartford	Policy Development & Planning Division CT Office of Policy & Management Hartford (203) 566-8285	Res. & Info., Employment Security Division Connecticut Dept. of Labor Wethersfield (203) 566-2120
Delaware	Delaware State College Jason Library Dover	Delaware Development Office Dover (302) 739-4271	Office of Occupational & Labor Market Information Delaware Department of Labor Newark (302) 368-6962

District of Columbia	Dept. of Commerce Library Washington	Mayor's Office of Planning Data Services Division Washington (202) 727-6533	Labor Market Information Department of Employment Services Washington (202) 639-1642
Florida	University of Florida Libraries Gainesville	Florida State Data Center Office of Planning & Budgeting Tallahassee (904) 487-2814	Bureau of Labor Market Information Dept. of Labor & Employment Security Tallahassee (904) 488-1048
Georgia	University of Georgia Libraries Athens	Div. of Demographic & Stat Services Georgia Office of Planning & Budget Atlanta (404) 656-0911	Labor Information Systems Department of Labor Atlanta (404) 656-3177
Guam	University of Guam Robert F. Kennedy Memorial Library Mangilao	Guam Department of Commerce Tamuning (671) 646-5841	
Hawaii	University of Hawaii Hamilton Library Honolulu	Dept. of Business, Econ. Development, & Tourism Honolulu (808) 536-2493	Research & Statistics Office Dept. of Labor & Industrial Relations Honolulu (808) 968-8999

Continued

State or Territory	Federal Depository Library[a]	State Data Center	BLS Cooperating State Agency
Idaho	University of Idaho Library Moscow	Idaho Department of Commerce Boise (208) 334-2470	Research & Analysis Department of Employment Boise (208) 334-6169
Illinois	Illinois State Library Springfield	Illinois State Data Center Illinois Bureau of the Budget Springfield (217) 782-1381	Economic Information & Analysis Dept. of Employment Security Chicago (312) 793-2316
Indiana	Indiana State Library Indianapolis	Indiana State Data Center Indiana State Library Indianapolis (317) 232-3733	Labor Market Information Dept. of Employment & Training Services Indianapolis (317) 232-8456
Iowa	University of Iowa Libraries Iowa City	Census Services Iowa State University Ames (515) 294-8337	Audit and Analysis Department Department of Employment Service Des Moines (515) 281-8181

Kansas	Gov't. Documents & Map Library Lawrence	State Library Topeka (913) 296-3295	Labor Market Information Services Department of Human Resources Topeka (913) 296-5058
Kentucky	Univ. of Kentucky Libraries Lexington	Center for Urban & Economic Research University of Louisville Louisville (502) 588-7990	Labor Market Research & Analysis Department of Employment Services Frankfort (502) 564-7976
Louisiana	LA State University Middleton Library Baton Rouge	Office of Planning & Budget Division of Administration Baton Rouge (504) 342-7410	Research & Statistics Division Dept. of Employment and Training Baton Rouge (504) 342-3141
Maine	University of Maine Fogler Library Orono	Division of Econ. Analysis & Research Maine Department of Labor Augusta (207) 287-2271	Division of Economic Analysis & Research Maine Department of Labor Augusta (207) 289-2271
Maryland	University of Maryland Hornbake Library College Park	Maryland Dept. of State Planning Baltimore (410) 225-4450	Office of Labor Market Analysis & Information Dept. of Econ. & Employment Devel. Baltimore (301) 333-5000

Continued

117

Appendix D   *Continued*

State or Territory	Federal Depository Library[a]	State Data Center	BLS Cooperating State Agency
Massachusetts	Boston Public Library Boston	MA Inst. for Social & Economic Research University of Massachusetts Amherst (413) 545-3460	Division of Employment Security Boston (617) 727-6868
Michigan	Michigan State Library Lansing	Michigan Information Center Dept. of Management & Budget Lansing (517) 373-7910	Bureau of Research & Statistics Employment Security Commission Detroit (313) 876-5445
Minnesota	University of Minnesota Wilson Library Minneapolis	Minnesota Planning State Demographer's Office St. Paul (612) 296-2557	Research & Statistical Services Dept. of Jobs and Training St. Paul (612) 296-6546
Mississippi	University of Mississippi Williams Library University	Center for Population Studies University of Mississippi University (601) 232-7288	Labor Market Information Dept. Employment Security Commission Jackson (601) 961-7424

Missouri	Univ. of Missouri—Columbia Ellis Library Columbia	Missouri State Library Jefferson City (314) 751-1823	Research and Analysis Division of Employment Security Jefferson City (314) 751-3591
Montana	University of Montana Mansfield Library Missoula	Census and Economic Info. Center Montana Department of Commerce Helena (405) 444-2896	Research and Analysis Department of Labor & Industry Helena (406) 444-2430
Nebraska	Univ. of Nebraska—Lincoln Love Memorial Library Lincoln	Center for Public Affairs Research University of Nebraska—Omaha Omaha (402) 595-2311	Labor Market Information Department of Labor Lincoln (402) 471-9964
Nevada	University of Nevada Library Reno	Nevada State Library Capitol Complex Carson City (702) 687-8327	Employment Security Research Employment Security Department Carson City (702) 687-4550
New Hampshire	New Hampshire State Library Concord	Office of State Planning Concord (603) 271-2155	Labor Market Information Department of Employment Security Concord (603) 228-4123

Continued

Appendix D *Continued*

State or Territory	Federal Depository Library[a]	State Data Center	BLS Cooperating State Agency
New Jersey	Newark Public Library Newark	New Jersey Department of Labor Division of Labor Market & Demographic Research Trenton (609) 984-2593	Labor Market and Demographic Research New Jersey Department of Labor Trenton (609) 292-0099
New Mexico	New Mexico State Library Santa Fe	Bureau of Business & Economic Research University of New Mexico Albuquerque (505) 277-2216	Economic Research and Analysis Bureau New Mexico Department of Labor Albuquerque (505) 841-8645
New York	New York State Library Albany	Division of Policy and Research Dept. of Economic Development Albany (518) 474-1141	Division of Research and Statistics New York State Dept. of Labor Albany (518) 457-6181
North Carolina	U of NC—Chapel Hill Davis Library Chapel Hill	State Data Center NC Office of State Planning Raleigh (919) 733-3683	Labor Market Information Division Employment Security Commission Raleigh (919) 733-2936

North Dakota	ND State University Library Fargo	Department of Agricultural Economics North Dakota State University Fargo (701) 237-8621	Research and Statistics Job Service of North Dakota Bismarck (701) 224-2868
Ohio	State Library of Ohio Columbus	Ohio Data Users Center Ohio Department of Development Columbus (514) 466-2115	Labor Market Information Division Bureau of Employment Services Columbus (614) 644-2689
Oklahoma	Oklahoma Dept. of Libraries Oklahoma City	Oklahoma State Data Center Oklahoma Department of Commerce Oklahoma City (405) 841-5184	Research Division Employment Security Commission Oklahoma City (405) 557-7116
Oregon	Portland State University Millar Library Portland	Center for Population Research & Census Portland State University Portland (503) 725-5159	Research and Statistics Oregon Employment Division Salem (503) 378-3220
Pennsylvania	State Library of Pennsylvania Harrisburg	Pennsylvania State Data Center Institute of State and Regional Affairs Pennsylvania State University at Harrisburg Harrisburg (717) 948-6336	Bureau of Research and Statistics Department of Labor and Industry Harrisburg (717) 787-3266

Continued

Appendix D *Continued*

State or Territory	Federal Depository Library[a]	State Data Center	BLS Cooperating State Agency
Puerto Rico	University of Puerto Rico Lazaro Library Rio Piedras	Puerto Rico Planning Board Minillas Government Center San Juan (809) 728-4430	Research and Statistics Division Dept. of Labor & Human Resources Hato Rey (809) 754-5385
Rhode Island	Rhode Island State Library Providence	RI Dept. of Administration Office of Municipal Affairs Providence (401) 277-6493	Labor Market Information and Management Services Dept. of Employment and Training Providence (401) 277-3730
South Carolina	Clemson University Library Clemson	Division of Research & Stat. Services South Carolina Budget & Control Board Columbia (803) 734-3780	Labor Market Information Employment Security Commission Columbia (803) 737-2660
South Dakota	South Dakota State Library Pierre	Business Research Bureau University of South Dakota Vermillion (605) 677-5287	Labor Market Information Center Department of Labor Aberdeen (605) 622-2314

Tennessee	Memphis State Univ. Libraries Memphis	Tennessee State Planning Office Nashville (615) 741-1676	Research & Statistics Division Dept. of Employment Security Nashville (615) 741-2284
Texas	Texas State Library Austin	Dept. of Rural Sociology Texas A & M University System College Station (409) 845-5115	Economic Research and Analysis Texas Employment Commission Austin (512) 463-2616
Utah	Utah State University Merrill Library Logan	Office of Planning and Budget Salt Lake City (801) 538-1550	Labor Market Information & Research Department of Employment Security Salt Lake City (801) 536-7400
Vermont	Vermont Dept. of Libraries Montpelier	Office of Policy Res. & Coordination Montpelier (802) 828-3326	Policy and Information Department of Employment & Training Montpelier (802) 229-0311
Virginia	University of Virginia Alderman Library Charlottesville	Virginia Employment Commission Richmond (804) 786-8308	Economic Information Services Virginia Employment Commission Richmond (804) 786-7496

Continued

Appendix D *Continued*

State or Territory	Federal Depository Library[a]	State Data Center	BLS Cooperating State Agency
Washington	Washington State Library Olympia	Forecasting Division Office of Financial Management Olympia (360) 586-2504	Labor Market Information Employment Security Department Olympia (360) 753-5114
West Virginia	W. Virginia University Library Morgantown	West Virginia Development Office Research & Strategic Planning Division Charleston (304) 558-4010	Labor and Economic Research Bureau of Employment Programs Charleston (304) 558-2660
Wisconsin	State Historical Society Library Madison	Demographic Services Center Department of Administration Madison (608) 266-1927	Labor Market Information Bureau Department of Industry, Labor and Human Relations Madison (608) 266-5843
Wyoming	Wyoming State Library Cheyenne	Survey Research Center University of Wyoming Laramie (307) 766-2931	Research and Planning Department of Employment Casper (307) 265-6715

[a]Other libraries in each state are also designated as Federal Depository Libraries. See *Census Catalog and Guide* for complete listing or call the depository library nearest you.

Appendix E   Census Bureau Regional Information Services and Special Topic Information Centers

Census Regional Offices: If you have questions about Census Bureau data, contact the regional office that serves your state (states served by each regional office are noted in parentheses). New York State is split between the Boston and New York offices.

Atlanta
101 Marietta St., NW
Atlanta, GA 30303-2700
(404) 730-3833
(AL, FL, GA)

Boston
2 Copley Pl., Suite 301
P.O. Box 9108
Boston, MA 02117-9108
(617) 424-0510
(CT, ME, MA, NH, NY, RI, VT)

Charlotte
901 Center Park Dr., Suite 106
Charlotte, NC 28217-2935
(704) 344-6144
(DC, KY, NC, SC, TN, VA)

Chicago
2255 Enterprise Dr., Suite 5501
West Chester, IL 60154-5800
(708) 562-1740
(IL, IN, WI)

Dallas
6303 Harry Hines Blvd., Room 210
Dallas, TX 75235-5269
(214) 767-7105
(LA, MS, TX)

Denver
6900 West Jefferson Ave., Suite 100
Lakewood, CO 80235
(303) 969-7750
(AZ, CO, NE, NM, ND, SD, UT, WY)

Detroit
1395 Brewery Park Blvd.
P.O. Box 33405
Detroit, MI 48232-5405
(313) 259-1875
(MI, OH, WV)

Kansas City
Gateway Tower II, Suite 600
400 State Ave.
Kansas City, KS 66101-2410
(913) 551-6711
(AR, IA, KS, MN, MO, OK)

Los Angeles
15350 Sherman Way, Suite 300
Van Nuys, CA 91406-4224
(818) 904-6339
(CA)

New York
Jacob K. Javits Federal Building,
Room 37-130
26 Federal Plaza
New York, NY 10278-0044
(212) 264-4730
(NY, NY City, Puerto Rico)

Philadelphia
105 South Seventh St., First Floor
Philadelphia, PA 19106-3395
(215) 597-8313
(DE, MD, NJ, PA)

Seattle
101 Stewart St., Suite 500
Seattle, WA 98101-1098
(206) 728-5314
(AK, HI, ID, MT, NV, OR, WA)

Special Data and Information Centers: The following organizations are associated with the National Census Information Center Program (NCIC).

Asian/Pacific Islander Data Consortium
Asian American Health Forum, Inc.
116 New Montgomery, Suite 531
San Francisco, CA 94105
(415) 541-0866

Indian Net Information Center
Department of Sociology
Henderson State University
1100 Henderson St.
Arkadelphia, AR 71923
(501) 246-5511, Ext. 3292

National Council of La Raza
810 First St., NE, Suite 300
Washington, DC 20002-4205
(202) 289-1380

National Urban League
1111 Fourteenth St., NW, 6th Floor
Washington, DC 20005
(202) 898-1604

Southwest Voter Research Institute
403 East Commerce
San Antonio, TX 78205
(210) 222-8014

Appendix F   Electronic Data Access

Many of the data sources discussed in this book are available electronically. Some can be accessed on electronic bulletin boards, usually for the cost of a phone call, and others require a commercial service user account. The following is a list of electronic access points for agencies that provide rural and nonmetro county data. For more details or further assistance, contact the sources below or your computer service provider.

The Federal Bulletin Board
The Federal BBS has numerous features, including online ordering capability for some information products; retrieval of product announcements, bibliographies, and other free bulletins; and thousands of files covering many government agencies. It is accessible via modem by dialing (202) 512-1387, or via Telnet through Internet to *Federal.bbs.gpo.gov 3001* (Port 3001). For more information, contact the GPO Office of Electronic Information Dissemination Services at (202) 512-1530.

Bureau of the Census
The Census Bureau Internet site and CENDATA can be accessed with three Internet applications: Gopher, World Wide Web, and anonymous File Transfer Protocol (FTP). For access:

(1)   Gopher client: On your local network, type *gopher gopher.census.gov*

(2)   World Wide Web: Use the Uniform Resource Locator (URL): *http://www.census.gov*

(3)   FTP: On your local network type *ftp ftp.census.gov*

Data users who do not have Internet access but do subscribe to CompuServe or DIALOG can also access the Census Bureau's CENDATA system. With CompuServe, type *GO CENDATA*; with DIALOG, type *BEGIN CENDATA*. See the *Census Catalog and Guide 1994* (pp. 5–7) for a list of menu options, or call: CompuServe at (800) 848-8199 or DIALOG Information Services, Inc. at (800) 334-2564.

E-mail comments or questions to *gatekeeper@census.gov*. Contact Jackson Morton at the Census Bureau's Public Information Office (*jmorton@census.gov*) or call (301) 457-2816 to get detailed instructions for accessing Internet and for receiving information from the Census Bureau's electronic mailing list.

Economic Research Service (ERS)

ERS data are available through the Albert R. Mann Library at Cornell University. For access:

(1) Gopher client: On your local network, type *gopher usda.mannlib. cornell.edu 70*

(2) Telnet: On your local network, type *telnet usda.mannlib.cornell. edu*; login as *usda*

(3) FTP: On your local network, type *ftp usda.mannlib.cornell.edu*; login as *anonymous* with your ID name or e-mail address as the password, then *cd usda*

Data users without Internet can access the ERS/NASS Bulletin Board. Dial (800) 821-6229 (communications settings N,8,1,F). For more detailed information about Internet access, contact Jim Horsfield (Room 724, 1301 New York Ave. NW, Washington, DC 20005-4788; (202) 219-0698; *jimh @ers.bitnet*)

National Agricultural Library ALF

To access the ALF electronic bulletin board directly, dial (301) 504-5496 or (301) 504-5497 (communications software settings N,8,1,F). To access ALF from Internet, follow these steps: *telnet fedworld.gov* (or IP Address 192.239.92.201); register on *Fedworld*; select *Gateway;* select *Gov't sys/database;* select *ALF.* The RIC can also be reached via the Internet *(ric @nalusda.gov)*.

Bureau of Labor Statistics

For access via FTP, type *stats.bls.gov;* register as *anonymous.*

For help, e-mail questions to *LABSTAT.Helpdesk@BLS.gov* or fax to (202) 606-7069. Non-Internet users can access BLS information through a bulletin board service for the price of the call by dialing (202) 606-7060.

References

1. Arizona Department of Economic Security, Research Administration, Population Statistics Unit. "Population Projections 1993–2040, Yavapai," February 1993.

2. Buse, Rueben C., and James L. Driscoll, editors. *Rural Information Systems: New Directions in Data Collection and Retrieval,* Iowa State University, Ames, 1992.

3. Cook, Annabel K. "Population Change in Local Areas," WREP 93, Western Rural Development Center, Oregon State University, Corvallis (undated).

4. Cook, Peggy J. and Karen L. Mizer. "The Revised ERS County Typology: An Overview," Rural Research Report 89, Rural Economy Division, Economic Research Service, U.S. Department of Agriculture, Washington, DC, December 1994.

5. Gold, Steven G. "The Federal Role in State Fiscal Stress," Center for the Study of the States, Nelson A. Rockefeller Institute of Government, State University of New York, Albany, June 1992.

6. Guralnik, David, Editor-in-Chief. *New World Dictionary: Second College Edition,* William Collins and World Publishing Co., Inc., New York, 1978.

7. Housing Assistance Council. "Taking Stock: Rural People and Poverty from 1970 to 1983," Washington, DC, 1984.

8. Iowa Agricultural Statistics. "1992 Agricultural Statistics," U.S. Department of Agriculture, National Agricultural Statistics Service, Iowa Office, Des Moines, March 1993.

9. Koebel, C. Theodore and Michael Price. "Kentucky Poverty Rates," in *Newsletter from the State Data Center of Kentucky,* Vol. 7, No. 1, Louisville, Kentucky, Winter 1989.

10. New Hampshire Office of State Planning. "Current Estimates and Trends in New Hampshire's Housing Supply, Update: 1992," Concord, New Hampshire, 1993.

11. O'Hare, William. "How to Evaluate Population Estimates," *American Demographics,* January 1988.

12. Plotnick, Robert D. "Rural Poverty in the Northwest: New Findings and Policy Implications," in *Northwest Report,* Northwest Area Foundation, No. 7, March 1989.

13. Robison, H.M., and Jon Freitag. "The Economic Impact to Local Communities of Eliminating the Wallowa–Whitman National Forest Timber Program," Center for Business Development and Research, University of Idaho, unpublished, 1994.

14. Ross, Christine M. and Sheldon Danziger. "Poverty Rates by State, 1979 and 1985: A Research Note," in *Focus,* Vol. 10, No. 3, Madison, Wisconsin, Fall 1987.

15. Salant, Priscilla and Paul Barkley. "Cost and Contract: Social Services in the Rural Northwest," Northwest Policy Center, University of Washington, Seattle, November 1993.

16. Salant, Priscilla and Don Dillman. *How to Conduct Your Own Survey,* John Wiley and Sons, New York, November 1994.

17. Salant, Priscilla and Julie Marx. *Small Towns, Big Picture,* Rural Economic Policy Program, Aspen Institute, Washington, DC, June 1995.

18. Shryock, Henry S., Jacob S. Siegel, and Associates. *The Methods and Materials of Demography,* Fourth Printing (Rev.), United States Department of Commerce, Washington, DC, June 1980.

19. Subcommittee on Intergovernmental Relations of the Committee on Governmental Affairs. "Governing the Heartland: Can Rural Governments Survive the Farm Crisis?" Committee Print 99–176, United States Government Printing Office, Washington, DC, 1986.

20. United States Department of Agriculture, Forest Service, Eastern Region. "Record of Decision, Final Environmental Impact Statement, Land and Resource Management Plan, White Mountain National Forest," April 1986.

21. United States Department of Agriculture, National Agricultural Library, Rural Information Center. "Update," July 1992.

22. United States Department of Commerce, Bureau of the Census. "American Housing Survey: Housing Data Between the Censuses," 1992.

23. _____. *Census Catalog and Guide: 1994,* May 1994.

24. _____. "Census '90 Basics," 1990 CPH-I-8, January 1990, revised April 1993.

25. _____. "Coast-to-Coast Digital Map Data Base for Arizona," 1993.

26. _____. *Compendium of Government Finances,* GC87(4)-5, April 1990.

27. _____. *Compendium of Public Employment,* GC87(3)-2, February 1991.

28. _____. *Consolidated Federal Funds Report: Fiscal Year 1993,* March 1994.

29. _____. *County and City Data Book,* 1994.

30. _____. *County Business Patterns,* CBP-92, selected issues, 1994.

31. _____. "Data for Communities," Census Factfinder Number 22 (Rev.), October 1991.

32. _____. "Educator's Guide to the 1990 Census," D-3300 C, August 1988.

33. _____. *Estimates of Resident Population of States and Counties, 1990-1992,* CPR Series PPL-3, 1994.

34. _____. "A Guide to State and Local Census Geography," 1990 CPH-I-18, June 1993.

35. _____. *Government Organization,* GS92(1)-1, March 1994.

36. _____. "Maps and More: Your Guide to Census Bureau Geography," July 1992, revised April 1994.

37. _____. *Population Estimates for Counties, July 1, 1992,* CPR Series PPL-7, February 1994.

38. _____. *Population Estimates for Counties and Metropolitan Areas: July 1, 1991,* CPR Series P-25 No. 1108, February 1994.

39. _____. "Preview of the 1992 Economic Census," EC92-PR-1, undated.

40. _____. *1987 Census of Mineral Industries,* MIC87-A-5, 1990.

41. _____. "1990 Census Facts," internal Census Bureau memo released November 9, 1992.

42. _____. *1990 Census of Population, Social and Economic Characteristics,* CP90-2, selected issues and CD-ROM, 1993.

43. _____. *1992 Census of Service Industries,* SC92-A-3, 1994.

44. United States Department of Commerce, Bureau of Economic Analysis. *Local Area Personal Income:1969–1992,* 1994.

45. _____. *Regional Economic Information System, 1969–1992,* CD-ROM, May 1994.

46. United States Department of Labor, Bureau of Labor Statistics. *Major Programs of the Bureau of Labor Statistics,* Report 871, May 1994.

47. _____. *Supplement to Unemployment in States and Local Areas, 1992,* issues on microfiche, May 1993.

48. Weber, Bruce A., Emery N. Castle, and Ann L. Shriver. "The Performance of Natural Resource Industries," in *Rural Economic Development for the 1980s,* Economic Research Service Staff Report AGES870724, July 1987.

49. West Virginia Bureau of Employment Programs. *Employment and Wages,* LER-LMI 201, Charleston, May 1994.

Index